BUILDING STRONG BONES & MUSCLES

Dr. Graham J. Fishburne

Dr. Heather Anne McKay

Stephen P. Berg, MEd

Human Kinetics

Library of Congress Cataloging-in-Publication Data

Fishburne, Graham J.
  Building strong bones & muscles / Graham J. Fishburne, Heather Anne
McKay, Stephen P. Berg.
    p. cm.
  Includes bibliographical references.
  ISBN 0-7360-4486-8 (softcover)
  1. Physical education and training--Study and teaching (Elementary)
I. McKay, Heather Anne, 1954- II. Berg, Stephen P., 1973- III. Title.
  GV363.F57 2005
  372.86--dc22

                                                    2005005905

ISBN: 0-7360-4486-8

The Web addresses cited in this text were current as of May 25, 2005, unless otherwise noted.

Acquisitions Editor: Bonnie Pettifor; **Developmental Editor:** Jennifer M. Sekosky; **Assistant Editors:** Ragen E. Sanner, Bethany J. Bentley, Carmel Sielicki; **Copyeditor:** John Wentworth; **Proofreader:** Julie Marx Goodreau; **Permission Manager:** Dalene Reeder; **Graphic Designer:** Fred Starbird; **Graphic Artist:** Dawn Sills; **Photo Managers:** Kelly J. Huff, Sarah Ritz; **Cover Designer:** Keith Blomberg; **Photographer (cover):** Dan Wendt; **Photographer (interior):** Dan Wendt, unless otherwise noted; **Art Manager:** Kelly Hendren; **Illustrator:** Tim Offenstein; **Printer:** Versa Press

Printed in the United States of America 10 9 8 7 6 5 4 3 2 1

Human Kinetics
Web site: www.HumanKinetics.com

United States: Human Kinetics
P.O. Box 5076
Champaign, IL 61825-5076
800-747-4457
e-mail: humank@hkusa.com

Canada: Human Kinetics
475 Devonshire Road Unit 100
Windsor, ON N8Y 2L5
800-465-7301 (in Canada only)
e-mail: orders@hkcanada.com

Europe: Human Kinetics
107 Bradford Road
Stanningley
Leeds LS28 6AT, United Kingdom
+44 (0) 113 255 5665
e-mail: hk@hkeurope.com

Australia: Human Kinetics
57A Price Avenue
Lower Mitcham, South Australia 5062
08 8277 1555
e-mail: liaw@hkaustralia.com

New Zealand: Human Kinetics
Division of Sports Distributors NZ Ltd.
P.O. Box 300 226 Albany
North Shore City
Auckland
0064 9 448 1207
e-mail: info@humankinetics.co.nz

CONTENTS

CHAPTER 1

CIRCUIT AND STATION ACTIVITIES   1

CHAPTER 2

GAME ACTIVITIES   47

CHAPTER 3

INSTRUCTIONAL GYMNASTICS ACTIVITIES   77

CHAPTER 4

DANCE ACTIVITIES   107

CHAPTER 5

SUPPLEMENTAL ACTIVITIES   125

ACTIVITY FINDER

Activities	Page number	Healthy bones	Muscular strength	Cardiovascular endurance	Flexibility	Cooperation	Agility	Balance	Skills and coordination
Chapter 1: Circuit and Station Activities									
Developmental Level 1									
Animal Exploration	5	x	x	x			x		x
Circus Circuit	7	x	x		x		x	x	x
Fitness Medley	9	x	x	x				x	x
Simple Circuit	11	x	x	x			x		x
Developmental Level 2									
Jump to It!	13	x	x	x					x
Muscle-Building Circuit	15	x	x	x					x
Olympic Events Circuit	17	x	x	x	x		x	x	x
Healthy Bones Circuit Training 1	19	x	x	x			x		x
Developmental Level 3									
Healthy Bones Circuit Training 2	27	x	x	x			x		x
Healthy Bones Circuit Training 3	35	x	x	x			x		x
Blastoff!	43	x	x	x					x
Resistance Training	45	x	x			x			
Chapter 2: Game Activities									
Developmental Level 1									
Copy Cat	48	x	x						x
Frogs and Grasshoppers	49	x	x						x
Jump the Snake	50	x	x						x
Leap the Brook	51	x	x						x
Leaping Lily Pads	52	x	x						x
Line Tag	54	x	x						x
Puddles in the Spring	55	x	x						x
Roll and Jump	56	x	x				x		x

(continued)

Activity Finder   *(continued)*

PREFACE

This book provides a selection of developmentally appropriate physical activities for young children. It contains games, exercises, and physical activities chosen and designed specifically to develop strong bones and muscles. Although the activities have been developed for children, people of all ages can use the activities to strengthen their bones and muscles. The activities will also improve many other important areas associated with a child's growth and development. For example, the activities promote cardiovascular fitness (the ability of the heart, lungs, and circulatory system to continue working efficiently over time), flexibility (the ability of muscles, tendons, and ligaments to reach a full range of motion), agility (the ability of muscles to respond quickly and fluidly), muscular endurance (the ability of a muscle or group of muscles to continue to function over an extended period of time), and other areas of physical fitness and well-being. Further, the activities provide practice opportunities to help develop basic movement and sport skills, and to learn movement concepts. They also aid in the development of cooperation among individuals within a group and the knowledge and understanding necessary for participation in active, healthy lifestyles.

Importance of Physical Activity

Physical activity plays an important role in a child's life. Children need to be engaged in regular physical activity to grow and develop to their full potentials. Leading a sedentary or inactive lifestyle is not healthy and can lead to many problems. Physical activity is essential for building strong bones and muscles.

The Need for Strong Bones

Strong bones are important to all of us. Bones form our skeleton, which protects our vital organs. With the help of muscles and other tissues, the skeleton is able to move so that we can experience life. Bones are considered healthy when their shape, structure, and density make them strong enough to withstand a whole range of activities without breaking. In childhod, this includes all of the daily locomotor, non-locomotor, and manipulative activities in which children engage. This is called "bone health." Healthy bones have a high amount of bone strength (the amount of force a bone can withstand without fracturing). When bones become weak through aging, disuse, or poor diet, they can break, which causes problems in movement and might affect the shape or posture of the skeleton. It has been estimated that bone fractures cost over $17 billion per year ($48 million per day) in the United States (Surgeon General's Report, 2004) and over $1 billion per year in Canada (Osteoporosis Society of Canada, 2004).

Adult bones are a product of the amount of bone gained during childhood and the amount lost with advancing age. If children attain an optimal bone mass during childhood and adolescence, this may well be the best protection against bone loss later in life.

Think of the skeleton as a bone bank. Deposits into the bone bank are made to replenish and constantly renew the skeleton. Bones are not lifeless structures; they are in fact living tissue in a constant state of change. They act as a storage reservoir for calcium and other minerals. Withdrawals from the bone bank are made as part of the natural process of renewal to overcome wear and tear. At the same time, withdrawals are made if the body needs to access calcium and other mineral deposits stored in the bone. These deposits and withdrawals from our "bone bank account" continue through life, and ideally we will make more deposits than withdrawals so that our savings add up! Physical activity and a healthy diet play crucial roles in determining the "bone balance" of our bone bank account. If either is lacking, our bone bank account begins to deplete, and the strength and health of our bones begin to pay the price. Research has shown that the elementary school years are an ideal time to make deposits into the bone bank account (McKay & Khan, 2000).

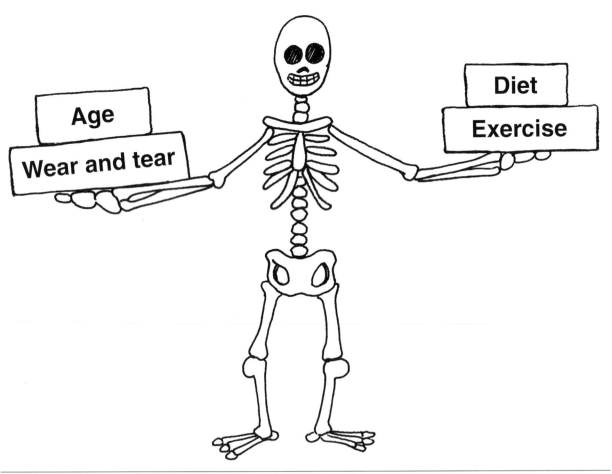

When bone savings are needed later in life, will there be enough stored away to meet the demand? Childhood is a time when greater benefits are achieved for the same investment. During the growing years, the skeleton is very responsive to exercise, and bone deposits can be more easily made to build up the bone bank account and promote a strong and healthy skeleton.

Bone is lost as a natural function of aging. The rate at which such loss occurs is based on genetics, hormones, and lifestyle factors—most importantly, diet and exercise. Bone is also lost very rapidly during periods of disuse. Consider astronauts who travel to space and live in the absence of earth's gravity and thus do not have any weight-bearing load on their bones for weeks or months. Without the stimulus of weight bearing, their bone bank balance is upset because more bone is lost than gained during their time in space. A similar scenario is observed during long periods of bed rest or immobilization after an accident or injury. The delicate balance involved in the "takeaway" (withdrawal) and "rebuild" (deposit) cycle of the bone is often affected. The balance starts to tip toward taking slightly more out of the bone than is deposited to replace it. This leads to a condition known as osteoporosis.

Osteoporosis

Osteoporosis is a bone disease that produces low bone mass through a deterioration of bone mass and structure. The disease is a consequence of removing more bone than is replaced. As we have already described, this process results in a negative bone balance that leads to bone fragility and a lack of bone strength. Thus, if a person with osteoporosis falls, he or she might more easily sustain a fracture, typically at the hip, spine, or wrist. Osteoporosis is often called "the silent thief" because the internal strength of bones is quietly stolen—a person might not even know he or she has osteoporosis until a fragile bone fractures.

It is estimated that over 44 million people in the United States are affected by osteoporosis and low bone mass. It is a common health problem in Canada as well, where an estimated 1.4 million people are affected. Osteoporosis affects people of all ethnic backgrounds, and the health care costs associated with fractures are extremely high. Of gravest concern, perhaps, are hip fractures because they require hospitalization and surgery that might result in long-term disability or even death. The U.S. Surgeon General's Report (2004) states that over 300,000 hip fractures occur in the United States each year, and it is estimated that about 70 percent of these are caused by osteoporosis. Hip fractures result in death in up to 20 percent of cases and in disability in 50 percent of those who survive. The report also noted that if preventive measures are not taken, by the year 2020 one in two Americans over age 50 will be at risk for fractures from osteoporosis or low bone mass. One of the myths associated with low bone mass and osteoporosis is that only women need to worry about bone health. Osteoporosis affects men and women of all races. The Surgeon General's Report (2004) is a call for everyone to take action to improve and maintain healthy bones. The report states that bone weakness manifests in older people and that strong bones begin in childhood.

Bone Strength Development

Many factors contribute to the development of a healthy skeleton, but physical activity is the key. Maintaining a balanced diet that includes adequate amounts of calcium and vitamin D is also very important. Approximately 26 percent of adult bone mass is attained in just two years during the adolescent height spurt! To put this into perspective, the amount of bone mass developed during this two-year period is as much bone mass as is typically lost during our entire adult life (Bailey, Faulkner, & McKay, 1996). Further, it has been estimated that over 98 percent of total bone mass has been attained by the time a student graduates from high school. Clearly, childhood and adolescence are important times to invest in bone health. The elementary school years provide a window of opportunity during which growing bone appears to respond more positively to physical activity than at any other time in life (MacKelvie, McKay, Petit, Moran, & Khan, 2002). The early years of schooling are a particularly good time to make rich deposits into the bone bank!

Dr. Heather McKay and her colleagues at the University of British Columbia in Canada conducted a series of exercise studies with children to see whether a simple program of weight-bearing activities could promote bone health. Children in "Healthy

Bones" schools were compared to children attending schools that did not participate in the Healthy Bones program. Results from their research have been highlighted on *ABC News World, Good Morning America,* and the Canadian Broadcasting Corporation. When children engaged in selected physical activities for as little as 5 to 10 minutes three times per week over one school year, bone structure and strength were enhanced (MacKelvie, McKay, Petit, Moran, & Kahn, 2002; McKay, Petit, Schutz, Prior, Barr, & Kahn, 2000). Furthermore, the benefits noted after the first year doubled for both boys and girls after a second year in the program. These Healthy Bones exercises, included in chapter 1, are easy for classroom teachers to deliver and can be done in the gym, the schoolyard, or the classroom.

It has recently been suggested that short, more frequent bouts of physical activity might be better for bone than intense, prolonged bouts of activity. Thus, Dr. McKay and colleagues conducted a study called "Bounce at the Bell" to assess whether bone health improved when jumping was performed by children in grades 4 and 5. Students performed between 5 and 12 jumps at the morning, noon, and last school bells, which took only a few minutes each day. Preliminary results showed that children in Bounce at the Bell schools significantly improved bone health compared to children who did not participate in the program (McKay, Tsang, Heinonen, MacKelvie, Sanderson, & Khan, 2005). We provide the Bounce at the Bell program in chapter 5.

These activities and the many other weight-bearing games and activities contained in this book will help develop strong bones and thus provide resistance to the bone-weakening disease osteoporosis.

The Need for Strong Muscles

Strong muscles go hand in hand with strong bones. As skeletal muscles contract, they impart a force on the bones to which they are connected. This relationship guides the most simple as well as the most complex movements that we perform every day in our lives. Regular participation in physical activity improves muscle strength and endurance, both considered important components of physical fitness. Over time, and with regular exposure to adequate physical activity, our muscular system adapts by increasing its strength and its ability to complete physical tasks.

Muscle strength and endurance allow us to perform our day-to-day tasks without undue stress, promote strong bones, facilitate movement and athletic performance, help to prevent injury to joints, and positively affect metabolism. If we encourage children and adolescents to develop and maintain strong muscles, we promote excellent lifelong physical activity habits and enhanced quality of life.

Muscle Strength Development

To enhance muscle strength, we must impose greater stresses on muscles than those to which they are already accustomed. For example, if a student walks to school regularly, to achieve a greater muscle strength benefit during this time he or she must run, skip, or perform some other physical activity with energy demands greater than walking. Muscle strength and endurance are enhanced (not surprisingly) only in those muscles called on to perform the work. Thus, activity programs that use as many muscle groups as possible are encouraged.

Just as physical activity promotes muscular strength and endurance, physical *inactivity* results in muscles that become weaker and shrink in size. Regular participation in the games and activities in this book provides an enjoyable means of building and maintaining strong muscles. Activities are presented at appropriate developmental levels to promote a safe pace for building muscle strength and endurance while avoiding injury.

National Standards

In addition to physical benefits, many educational benefits can be gained through participation in the activities we provide. If children engage in these games and activities during their school physical education classes they will be meeting many of the learning outcomes associated with their physical education curricula.

Throughout the world, many national, state, and provincial jurisdictions identify school physical education curricula for children. These curricula provide schools with descriptions of learning outcomes they expect children to achieve through participation in physical education. Typical learning outcomes include development of basic or fundamental movement skills (e.g., running, jumping, hopping, skipping, galloping), the learning of motor skills (e.g., throwing, catching, kicking), improved physical fitness, and development of the knowledge and attitudes necessary to lead active and healthy lifestyles. In the table that follows, we present a brief review of physical education curricula learning outcomes from several countries and various educational jurisdictions to show how the games and activities in this book address desired learning outcomes.

NATIONAL STANDARDS COMPARISON

Country	Standards	How *Building Strong Bones & Muscles* addresses these standards
Australia (Victoria)[a]	Movement and physical activity—Perform motor skills and movement patterns with proficiency	Many activities in this book promote locomotor, nonlocomotor, and manipulative skill development through a sequential, developmentally appropriate approach.
	Movement and physical activity—Identify the benefits of physical activity	Knowledge of physical activity and healthy bone and muscle development is covered and a variety of assessment strategies are provided to assess children's knowledge in this area.
	Health of individuals and populations—Identifying personal health goals	A variety of methods and ideas to help set personal goals to perform weight-bearing physical activities, participate in circuits, and so on are provided.
	Health of individuals and populations—Describing what it means to be healthy	Through completion of the activities contained in this book children will gain an understanding of many aspects of physical health and well-being.
Australia (Queensland)[b]	Developing concepts and skills for physical activity—Enhancing physical performance in games, sports, and other physical activities through monitoring and evaluating movement sequences and applying basic movement concepts	Through participating in developmentally appropriate games, dance, gymnastics, and circuit activities, children will enhance their physical performance while applying basic movement concepts to their physical activities. The variety of assessment methods covered provides ideas to help in the evaluation of movement sequences.

(continued)

Country	Standards	How *Building Strong Bones & Muscles* addresses these standards
Australia (New South Wales)[c]	Promote physical activity every day	By incorporating take-home activities and having a variety of games, dance, gymnastics, and circuit activities for school, children will be able to be physically active every day to help increase their muscular strength and optimize bone health.
	Factors influencing personal health choices	Children will learn how to develop and maintain bone and muscle strength by incorporating weight-bearing activities and healthy eating habits into their daily routines.
	The adoption of an active lifestyle	Children will benefit from weight-bearing activities and, ideally, will incorporate these types of activities into their personal lifestyles. Knowledge of healthy bone development, muscle strength, and personal physical fitness will help children gain an understanding of the importance of an active lifestyle.
	Fundamental movement patterns and coordinated actions of the body	This book provides developmentally appropriate games, dances, gymnastics, and circuit activities. Participation in these developmentally appropriate activities helps children develop a variety of important locomotor, nonlocomotor, and manipulative skills.
Western Australia[d]	Knowledge and understanding of health and physical activity concepts to lead active, healthy lifestyles	Children will gain a greater understanding of the physical activities and healthy lifestyle habits that lead to greater bone and muscle development.
	Skills for physical activity	Children will develop and perform fundamental motor patterns through developmentally appropriate activities. A wide variety of motor skills essential for physical activity and sports can be developed through participation in the activities covered in this book.
	Interpersonal skills	Some activities in the book are designed to have children work with others to gain interpersonal skills and understanding. In addition to the usual competitive game activities, cooperative activities are provided to help children develop these important skills.

Country	Standards	How *Building Strong Bones & Muscles* addresses these standards
Canada[e]	In Canada, each province regulates its own physical education curriculum program for its schools. However, the overall learning outcome across all provinces is to develop the skills, knowledge, and attitudes necessary to lead active, healthy lifestyles. The Canadian Association for Health, Physical Education, Recreation and Dance (CAHPERD) supports and promotes this overall learning objective.	The goal of this book is to provide children with developmentally appropriate activities that enhance bone and muscular strength. Through participation in these activities, children are provided with opportunities to develop strong bones and muscles, improve their overall physical fitness, and improve their physical skills and knowledge about healthy bones and muscles. The activities in this book provide children with opportunities to develop healthy attitudes toward physical activity.
Hong Kong[f] (Key Stages 1, 2, 3, and 4)	Motor and sports skills development	The activities contained in this book provide opportunities for children to engage in locomotor, nonlocomotor, and manipulative skills. Such skills form the basis or foundation for successful participation in many sports. All activities are presented in a sequential, developmentally appropriate manner.
	Health and fitness development	Activities are designed to enhance and develop an awareness of how bone and muscular strength are beneficial for overall health and physical well-being.
	Knowledge of movement	This book provides a wide variety of developmentally appropriate activities for the development of strong bones and muscles. While the activities are designed primarily to promote bone and muscle strength, children will also gain knowledge, skills, and positive attitudes toward active and efficient human movement.
United Kingdom[g] (Key Stages 1 and 2)	Acquiring and developing skills	Children will develop fundamental motor patterns and fundamental motor skills through the developmentally appropriate activities described in the book.
	Selecting and applying skills, tactics, and compositional ideas	Children will engage in weight-bearing activities individually, in pairs, and in small groups. Through participation in the games provided, children learn and apply a variety of skills and tactics.

(continued)

Country	Standards	How *Building Strong Bones & Muscles* addresses these standards
United Kingdom[g] (Key Stages 1 and 2) *(continued)*	Evaluating and improving performance	Children will participate in a variety of games, dances, and gymnastics activities. They will be given the opportunity to identify and assess their performances through personal goal setting, observation techniques, and other assessment strategies.
	Knowledge and understanding of fitness and health	Activities in this book are designed to promote and develop an awareness of how bone and muscular strength are beneficial for overall health and physical well-being.
United States[h]	Demonstrates competency in motor skills and movement patterns needed to perform a variety of physical activities	Children will develop fundamental motor skills through the developmentally appropriate activities provided. These fundamental skills form the basis on which many other skills are built and developed as children participate and engage in sports and physical activity.
	Demonstrates understanding of movement concepts, principles, strategies, and tactics as they apply to the learning and performance of physical activities	Although the focus of the book is to promote bone and muscle development, children will receive other physical benefits, such as cardiovascular fitness, flexibility, agility, and balance skills.
	Participates regularly in physical activity	To motivate children to participate in regular physical activity, take-home activities and goal-setting strategies are included in the activity and lessons ideas presented in this book.
	Achieves and maintains a health-enhancing level of physical fitness	Activities in this book are designed to enhance and develop an awareness of how bone and muscle strength are beneficial to the overall health and physical well-being of an individual.
	Exhibits responsible personal and social behavior that respects self and others in physical activity settings	Many of the activities in this book promote cooperative learning among children and foster respect through fair play. A feature of the text is the use of personal goal-setting techniques and the promotion and development of healthy lifestyle behaviors.

Country	Standards	How *Building Strong Bones & Muscles* addresses these standards
United States *(continued)*	Values physical activity for health, enjoyment, challenge, self-expression, and/or social interaction	Through participation in the activities covered in this book children will increase their knowledge and understanding of the importance of regular physical education and physical activity in their daily lives. They will learn that strong bones and muscles developed early in life will be very important to offset bone degeneration and loss of mobility later in life.

[a]Adapted, by permission, from the Victorian Curriculum Assessment Authority, 2004. www.vcaa.vic.edu.au. Assessed 11/4/04.
[b]Queensland School Curriculum Council (now the Queensland Study Authority), *Years 1 to 10 Health and Physical Education Syllabus,* 1999, Brisbane, Australia. www.qsa.qld.edu.au. Assessed 10/13/05.
[c]PDHPE K-6 Syllabus © Board of Studies NSW for and on behalf of the Crown in right of the State of New South Wales, 1999.
[d]Adapted, by permission, from the Curriculum Council Government of Western Australia. www.curriculum.wa.edu.au/pages/framework/framework06b.htm. Assessed 10/13/04.
[e]www.cahperd.ca
[f]By permission of the Education and Manpower Bureau, Government of the Hong Kong Special Administrative Region.
[g]Reprinted, by permission, from the Qualifications and Curriculum Authority, http://www.nc.uk.net.
[h]Reprinted from *Moving Into the Future: National Standards for Physical Education,* 2nd Edition (2004) with permission from the National Association for Sport and Physical Education (NAPSE), 1900 Association Drive, Reston, VA 20191-1899.

Summary

During the early years, when children are growing and developing, it is essential that they engage in physical activities that will help them develop strong bones and muscles. Research studies have shown that bones need to be subjected to weight-bearing activities to facilitate growth and development. Physical activity can provide opportunities for weight-bearing activity. Regular physical activity is also needed for proper muscle, tendon, and ligament development. It is essential during the early growing years that children engage in the types of exercise and physical activity that maximize growth and development of muscles and bones. This book provides guidance for "best practices." That is, it identifies developmentally appropriate exercises and physical activities for children and youth—exercises and activities that have been shown through research studies to significantly increase bone strength and promote muscle development.

ACKNOWLEDGMENTS

We would like to thank Dr. Moira A. Petit, Dr. Kerry J. MacKelvie, Heather Macdonald (PhD candidate), Kate Reed (PhD candidate) and Leslie Bryant McLean (MSc) for their contribution to the design of the Healthy Bones, Bounce at the Bell, and Action Schools! BC programs, and for conducting the studies that measured their effectiveness.

A big thank you to all the students, principals, staff, teachers and parents in the Richmond and Vancouver School Districts, British Columbia, Canada who participated in the Healthy Bones, Bounce at the Bell and Action Schools! BC studies. We could not have done this without all of you.

We acknowledge and are grateful for the generous support from the Michael Smith Foundation for Health Research, Canadian Institutes for Health Research, the BC Ministry of Health Services and 2010 Legacies Now Corporation. The evaluation of the Healthy Bones and Bounce at the Bell programs was conducted under the auspices of the Department of Orthopedics, University of British Columbia and the Vancouver Coastal Health Research Institute.

Finally, we would like to acknowledge the talent of Ryland Haggis who provided the concept design for the figures on the Activity Cards. Many thanks for your contribution.

HOW TO USE THIS BOOK

The games and activities contained in this book can be put to use in many ways. If teachers choose to use the activities in a school setting, some components may be adopted as a regular 5- to 10-minute bone and muscle strength and fitness component. Activities can also be completed as a warm-up to physical education class. Or they can be done in a regular classroom setting during a short fitness break.

The games and activities can also be incorporated into regular physical education classes. Activities have been designed to encompass a vast number of curricular learning outcomes, beyond bone and muscle development. We provide ideas for how teachers might achieve integration across curricular areas and how lessons about healthy bones and muscles can be reinforced through activities presented in other classes. For example, the game Animal Exploration in chapter 1 teaches children about the movements of animals and can be used either independently or as part of a unit on nature and animals. Working with teachers of other subject areas helps develop the cross-curricular possibilities for these activities.

Of course, the games and activities can also be used outside of a school program. This might include healthy bone and muscle initiatives for the entire school or community programs that guide children toward daily physical activity and the development of an active, healthy lifestyle.

Organizing the Classroom

To aid you with the setup and delivery of exercises, we recommend using assessment and task cards, and we have included suggestions for creating these. We also recommend creating and using station signs.

• **How to Create and Use Station Signs.** Stations and circuits (described in chapter 1) are used throughout the book. Station signs are created to indicate names of station activities and posted at the designated station within a circuit. As children move through the circuit from station to station, they will find a sign at each station giving the name of the exercise or activity to be completed there. For example, in the Animal Exploration circuit in chapter 1, seven station signs guide children to and from seven animal stations: Crab Walk, Kangaroo Corner, Cheetah Sprint, Seal Rock, Swinging Monkeys, Grizzly Bear Grotto, and Squirmy Snakes.

• **How to Create and Use Activity Cards.** Activity cards accompany some of the activities and exercises described in the book (Healthy Bones Circuit Training 1, 2, and 3 in chapter 1 and Bounce at the Bell in chapter 5). These cards, which help in the setup and delivery of activities, can easily be created for activities that do not already have them. The cards provide descriptions of the activities and the actions required to do them. Detailed descriptions accompany all the activities and exercises presented in this book, and these can be used to create activity cards appropriate for the developmental level of the children completing the activities. An activity card placed at each station provides the child with a description of how the station's activity is to be done. For an example, see the activity card on the next page for the Crab Walk station.

• **How to Create and Use Task Cards.** Task cards are used to set tasks for individual children to complete. These cards help individualize activities to the developmental level of each child. Children carry their own personal task cards from station to station. When they arrive at a station sign, they first read the activity card to understand what activity action is required. Each child then consults his or her own personal task card to determine the task (or achievement goal) that has been set for him or her to complete at this station. In addition to identifying developmentally appropriate tasks, task cards can be used in goal setting to help stimulate children. Goal setting can be a very effective method to motivate children to reach achievable standards, especially if the child is personally involved in setting the achievement goals. For an example of what a child's task card might say, see the sample task card below for the Animal Exploration circuit's Crab Walk station.

- **Ideas for Assessment.** Task cards and activity cards create a mechanism to engage children in the exercises and activities designed to help them develop strong bones and muscles. It is important to assess how well children are completing the tasks they have been set. Several ideas and methods to help assess completion and quality of performance associated with the tasks can be found in appendix B.

- **Ideas for a Cross-Curricular Approach.** Many of the activities, games, and dances coordinate well with lessons in other subject areas. Some ideas for cross-curricular lesson development have been listed with the variations and are designed to correspond with the developmental levels of the activity. Appendix A includes reproducible materials for classroom learning activities.

CRAB WALK ACTIVITY CARD

Walking on their hands and feet, with bellies facing the ceiling, children crab walk around four cones, moving either forward, sideways, or backward. (Providing an illustration or picture of the Crab Walk is recommended. A picture is helpful to all children, especially to those at a lower level of reading comprehension.)

TASK CARD   **Name of Child: I. M. Fit**

ANIMAL EXPLORATION CIRCUIT

Crab Walk station

Week 1—Crab walk around the four cones twice.

Week 2—Crab walk around the four cones three times.

Week 3—Crab walk around the four cones four times.

Seal Rock station

Week 1—(and so on)

Organization of Activities

The games, exercises, and physical activities presented in this book have been organized to aid you in your use and selection of them. Icons, developmental levels, and the layout of the activities help you find the activity most appropriate for your needs.

Key to Icons

Icons are used throughout the book to identify major learning outcomes or benefits associated with an activity. When choosing an activity, you will know by the accompanying icon exactly what benefits the child will receive through participation in the activity.

1	2	3	4	5	6	7	8
Healthy Bones	Muscular Strength	Cardiovascular Endurance	Flexibility	Cooperation	Agility	Balance	Skills and Coordination

Developmental Levels

When engaging in physical activity, children should perform at a level appropriate to their current level of physical development and fitness. Often, children try to engage in too much too soon by placing themselves in situations that require them to perform beyond their level of ability. In such cases, their enjoyment is compromised, and they might get hurt. Thus, it is important to determine the appropriate developmental level of each child who undertakes a program of physical activity.

The activities in this book are organized into three developmental levels, which correspond approximately to the age groups listed here:

> **Developmental Level 1:** Early childhood, ages 5–7
>
> **Developmental Level 2:** Middle childhood, ages 8–9
>
> **Developmental Level 3:** Late childhood, ages 10–12

There are distinct cognitive, physical, and social–emotional differences among children at these three developmental levels. We have organized the games and activities in this book to provide for children in early, middle, or late childhood so that they might fully participate, avoid injury, and maximize their enjoyment.

Lesson Plan Template

All exercises and physical activities presented in this book follow the same layout and lesson plan format. This lesson plan template has been chosen to help describe each activity and to show how these activities can be used most effectively. The following is a list of the information included for each activity. These details should help you understand quickly what the activity is intended to do and if it is the right activity for the program you are planning.

- **Developmental Levels.** The appropriate level is identified for each lesson. This helps you select activities based on your needs.
- **Objectives.** The objectives list the muscular and skeletal benefits, movement skills, and concepts you can expect children to learn and achieve through participation in a particular activity.
- **Equipment Needed.** This section lists the equipment you will need for children to undertake an activity.
- **Setup.** This section may contain a diagram (see the key for diagrams that follows) or instructions for setting up participants within a space allotted for an activity.
- **Instructions.** This section contains detailed directions for what children should do during an activity and might include a list of exercises or dance steps to choose from.
- **Stations.** A list of exercise names and instructions for circuit stations are provided in this section.
- **Safety Considerations.** If an activity has anything unusual or special about it that might require some extra consideration regarding safety, such information is found in this section.
- **Variations.** The purpose of this section is to give you diverse opportunities to use the activity to the fullest. Options for ways to extend the activity or to introduce a cross-curricular element to the activity are detailed.
- **Assessment.** This part of the lesson offers suggestions to help you determine what children have learned and achieved by doing an activity.

Key for diagrams

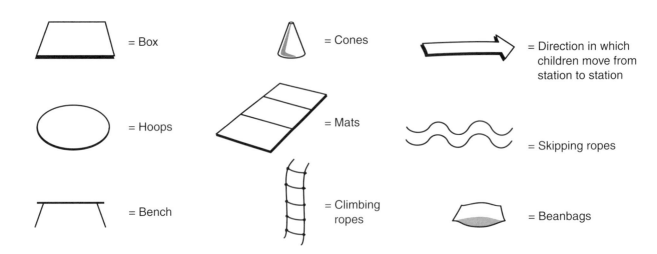

= Box

= Cones

= Direction in which children move from station to station

= Hoops

= Mats

= Skipping ropes

= Bench

= Climbing ropes

= Beanbags

Modifying Activities to Include All Children

The three developmental levels employed in this book are designed to allow children of different ages and stages of growth and development to complete activities successfully. However, these levels are just approximate—there will be children with other needs who, although they fall within the ages associated with the developmental level, will be operating either below or above the designated level. For example, a child with a developmental delay might not be able to participate successfully in activities associated with the developmental level corresponding to his or her chronological age. The instructional environment for this child will need to be individualized to allow him or her to experience success in the activity. Similarly, physically gifted children might be underchallenged at the developmental level that corresponds to their age. These children will need greater challenges to maintain motivation and push them toward realizing their full potential. To ensure that all children achieve the pleasure and feeling of success, it will sometimes be necessary to adjust activities to meet a number of children's individual and unique needs. Modifying activities to include all children, regardless of ability level, can be done. Generally, the ways to modify a learning situation involve changing the number of participants, changing the space you are working in, changing the rules of the activity, or changing the equipment (Fishburne, 2005).

- **Changing the number of participants.** If an activity involves many children participating at the same time, you might consider reducing the number of players. Having more players generally means more options and more decisions. Reducing the number of participants in a group helps reduce the complexity of the situation, and it also means more time on task—for example, more players will be able to touch the ball during a game. Reducing the number of players usually also reduces the number of choices, which helps the child who finds it difficult to experience success when the situation offers too many possibilities.

- **Changing the space.** Modifying the space in which an activity occurs can also raise success rates. For example, increasing the amount of space for a competitive game activity can provide children with more time to make decisions. Correct decisions or more time to complete movements often results in greater success. Reducing space usually results in more complexity for children.

- **Changing the rules.** If children are having difficulties with an activity, consider changing the activity's rules. For example, if an activity calls for 10 jumping jacks and 10 push-ups, you might instead require 5 jumping jacks and 10 modified push-ups.

- **Changing the equipment.** Changing the size of the ball, changing a juggling ball to a beanbag, changing a ball to a beach ball or balloon, or changing a type or size of a racket can all help increase the level of success for a child. If a child is having difficulty with equipment, consider ways to modify the equipment to allow the child to complete the task more easily. For example, if children are using resistance bands in their activities, make sure the tension of the bands suits the needs of the children performing the activities.

Our aim in this book is to provide developmentally appropriate activities to promote bone and muscular strength in children. If you can modify the activities to ensure they are individually appropriate for each child, then all children will reach the goal of becoming stronger and healthier.

This book provides a wide variety of exercises and activities for the development of strong bones and muscles. While these exercises and activities have been carefully chosen and designated developmentally appropriate, if you have a concern about the safety of any of the exercises or activities, do not use them. Use only the exercises and activities you are comfortable with.

Further, recognized safety procedures should be followed based on the safety rules and regulations in place in the jurisdiction or school district where the activities are to be undertaken. This may include using mats, wearing recommended clothing and footwear, and following certain routines and progressions. In order to show technique, mats are not shown in every photo; however, it is recommended to use them as much as possible in class. Check on the safety rules and regulations in your jurisdiction or school district before using any of the activities in this book.

© Human Kinetics

CHAPTER 1

CIRCUIT AND STATION ACTIVITIES

Stations and circuit activities can be effective methods of organizing children in the physical education setting. Among the many benefits associated with stations and circuits are that they are

fun,

interactive,

fast paced,

time efficient,

adaptable, and

progressive.

Thus, many physical educators find circuit and station activities ideal for the short instructional periods of physical education typical of elementary schools.

Station work involves a set number of practice areas within the gym or other instructional area. Children work at each station for either a set time or until they have completed a task, then they rotate to another station. Each station can be used for general fitness work, skill development, or practice. Whether using stations for fitness work or skill development, instructors should go through each station with the children to demonstrate the activity and cover safety and behavior issues.

The term "circuit training" is often used in association with physical fitness work and usually involves several fitness stations arranged in circuit formation. Like station work, circuit activities involve either repeating one or more exercises for a set number of repetitions or completing as many repetitions as possible within a set amount of time. Research has shown significant positive effects on bone health in children when a 10-minute circuit is completed three times per week and the level of difficulty is gradually increased over the course of a normal school year (McKay & Khan, 2000; MacKelvie, McKay, Petit, Moran, & Khan, 2002).

As noted previously, circuit and station work activities have many advantages. They are very adaptable and can be used as either starting activities or as part of an entire lesson. Circuit activities can also be adjusted to meet individual differences. If children follow their own achievable personalized goals at each station (written on a personal task card), then circuit activities can be individualized and developmentally appropriate for each child.

Maintaining and Increasing Strength and Fitness

If children participate in a circuit twice a week and perform the same number of repetitions at each station every time the circuit is completed, then levels of strength and fitness are maintained, which is a desirable outcome. However, it is often more desirable to gradually raise levels of strength and fitness, especially if children initially start the circuits with fairly low levels of strength and fitness.

For children to gradually increase their strength and fitness, they will need to work harder to complete the circuit, gradually increasing the amount of effort they put in. You can gradually increase the effort or amount of exercise required to complete a circuit in several ways:

- Increase the number of repetitions required at each station. For example, if children complete a circuit twice a week and four modified push-ups are required to complete one of the station activities, then in week 2 the number of required modified push-ups can be increased to five, and after that one more modified push-up can be added to the circuit every week, thus requiring children to work a little harder each week to complete the circuit. Note that requiring all children to complete the same number of repetitions at each station is usually not the most effective strategy because the children are not all at the same developmental level. Having each child complete task cards that set realistic personal goals that specify the number of repetitions to be completed at each station better accommodates the variety of developmental levels of the children. When appropriate—that is, when a child is completing existing circuit requirements without undue fatigue—repetitions should be increased. Likewise, if a certain number of repetitions is causing too much exertion or stress, the number should be immediately decreased to maintain a developmentally appropriate level of difficulty.

- Set a duration of time to spend at each station activity. Have children try to complete as many practices (repetitions) as they can within the specified time. Increase durations gradually, perhaps every two to three weeks, to require children to work slightly harder at each exercise station as they complete as many repetitions as they can within a longer time frame.

- Increase the number of circuit completions. If the circuit is to be completed twice a week, after the first two weeks, for example, increase the frequency to three times per week. The strength and fitness level of the children determines when an increase is suitable. If children can complete the circuit easily, without undue fatigue, it is probably time to increase frequency.

- Change station activities. Another way to increase the work and effort required at a station is to change the station's activity to one that requires more effort to complete.

IMPORTANT CONSIDERATIONS FOR CIRCUITS AND STATIONS

1. **Safety.** The safety of the children is the primary concern when involving them in stations or circuits. Ensure that each station or circuit is developmentally appropriate for the grade you are teaching and has been adjusted to meet the individual needs of each child. To reduce the risk of injury, ensure that children perform within their limits and do not overextend themselves. Safety concerns are most important when children are increasing levels of difficulty or number of repetitions or making other changes in a station activity. No matter what their developmental level, all children should be taught to engage safely in circuit activities. Be particularly careful with children engaging in circuit or station work for the first time. If a child is injured, stop the activity immediately and provide appropriate first aid.

2. **Warm-up.** To help guard against muscle strains and pulls, children should do warm-up activities and stretches before engaging in weight-bearing exercises. Light running or jogging should precede gentle stretching exercises. Light running helps promote blood flow in muscles before stretching.

3. **Progression and level of difficulty.** When using stations or circuits, make sure children start and progress at a comfortable level. It is best to start easy and build to more difficult levels gradually. If you see a child completing a circuit or station activity quite easily without undue fatigue, you can make changes to increase the difficulty level. Implement gradual changes throughout the year to increase the level of difficulty. In the circuits that follow, we offer suggestions about the number of repetitions to be completed. For example, we might suggest in the exercise activities to start with 5 repetitions and gradually build up to 10. However, as with all circuit activities, the number of repetitions can be set on an individual basis to correspond to the developmental level of the child participating in the circuit. Individual and realistic goal setting can be identified on a personal circuit task card. Children take their personal task cards with them from station to station and eventually increase the number of repetitions to correspond to their goals. Remember to begin at easier levels of difficulty and gradually build up to more difficult ones.

4. **Balance.** As a rule, if station 1 involves children performing lower body activities, such as hopping, have station 2 include more upper body activities, such as push-ups. This way the child works on strength and bone development while providing opportunities for major muscle groups to rest and recover between stations.

5. **Station sign.** In addition to explaining and demonstrating each station to children before they start the circuit, create a station sign for each station with a diagram and description of the station's activity.

6. **Music.** Using music to accompany circuit activities adds enjoyment and interest. Letting children select music to accompany the circuit helps motivate them to complete the exercise activities. The rhythm and beat of the music often dictate the speed at which children try to complete the circuit activities, so choose your music carefully.

Developmental Levels

The activities in each chapter are divided into three developmental levels (see How To Use This Book, page xix). Here are some suggestions for working with children at each level.

- **Developmental Level 1.** When performing fitness activities in stations or circuits, give children at this level frequent rest periods because they tend to have short, quick bursts of energy and tire quickly. However, children also recover quite quickly after a short rest period. Gradually increase the level of difficulty at each station throughout the year.

- **Developmental Level 2.** Children at this level show an increase in overall strength. Continue to give children frequent breaks between stations. Gradually increase the level of difficulty at each station throughout the year.

- **Developmental Level 3.** At this level, children show a continued increase in muscular strength, and station activities should provide for this. As in the first two developmental levels, give children frequent breaks between stations. Remember that children tend to tire easily but recover quickly. Gradually increase the level of difficulty at each station throughout the year.

ANIMAL EXPLORATION

Objectives

To improve bone strength, muscle strength, and jumping and climbing skills; to promote body awareness and transfer of weight

Equipment Needed

> Cones
> Floor mats
> Climbing ropes
> Station signs to indicate the name of the activity at each circuit station

Setup

We recommend organizing your stations in this order, as shown in the diagram: Crab Walk, Kangaroo Corner, Cheetah Sprint, Seal Rock, Swinging Monkeys, Grizzly Bear Grotto, and Squirmy Snakes.

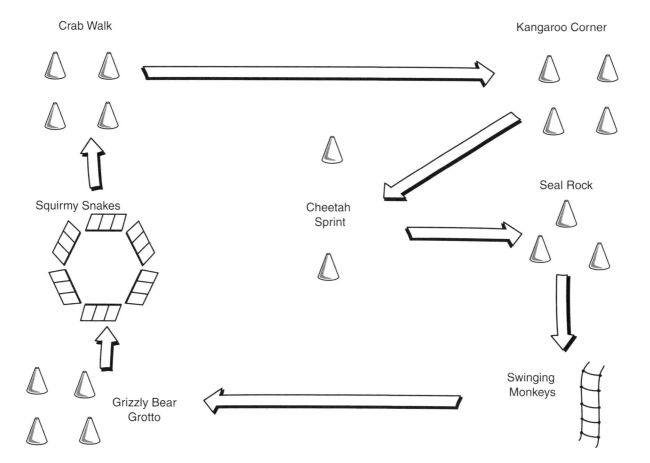

Instructions

The objective of Animal Exploration is to have children perform a different animal movement activity at several different stations. Rotate children from one station to the next every few minutes.

Stations

Crab Walk. Children crab walk around the four cones on their hands and feet; with their bellies facing the ceiling, they move forward, sideways, or backward.

Kangaroo Corner. Children jump with both feet together around the cones. For variation, place a ball or beanbag between their knees.

Cheetah Sprint. Children run quickly to and from designated cones, resting between runs.

Seal Rock. Children lie on the ground facedown; pushing their bodies up with their hands and arms, they walk with their hands, pulling themselves around the cones.

Swinging Monkeys. Children hang onto a climbing rope and swing. Make sure the maximum height allowed up the rope is specified (a ribbon can be tied on the rope to identify the maximum height). Children can also hang on the rope and make shapes. Place floor mats under the ropes for safety. If there are more children than ropes, organize the children to take turns.

Grizzly Bear Grotto. Children move around the cones on all fours, placing both hands on the floor with slightly bent legs.

Squirmy Snakes. Children lie on their bellies and slither from mat to mat, moving around the circle.

Safety Considerations

▷ Children must take turns at each station. For example, only one child at a time should be on a climbing rope.

▷ Place floor mats under climbing ropes.

▷ Ensure proper form of the movement activities before starting.

Variations

▷ Change the stations to accommodate different animal movements, such as a track for Galloping Horses.

▷ For a cross-curricular approach, use this activity as part of a unit on nature, animals, or geography.

Assessment

▷ Discuss the geographic locations of each animal.

▷ Ask children to identify the fastest and the slowest moving animals.

▷ Ask children to draw pictures depicting the movement of each animal and to label the body parts involved in the movements. Keep artwork in their assessment portfolios.

CIRCUS CIRCUIT

Objectives

To improve bone and muscle strength and bone development; to promote jumping, leaping, balancing, and rolling skills; to introduce children to the concept of weight transfer

Equipment Needed

> Balance beams or benches
> Floor mats
> Gymnastics box top
> Cones
> Beanbags
> Climbing ropes
> Scooters
> Jump ropes
> Station signs to indicate the name of the activity at each circuit station

Setup

We recommend organizing your stations in this order, as shown in the diagram: Clown Cars, Tightrope Walker, Cannonball, Mule Kicks, Rolly Polly Clown, Trapeze Artist, and Lion Jumps.

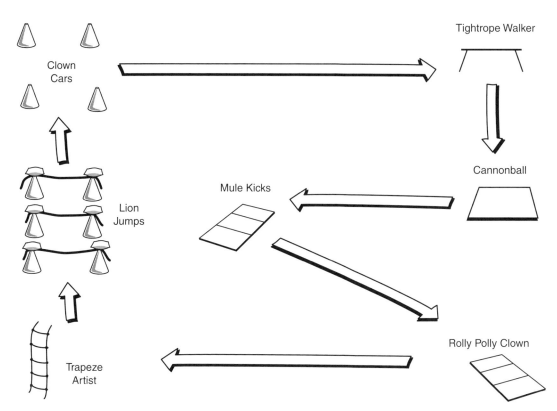

Instructions

Children rotate through several stations.

Stations

Clown Cars. Children sit on small gymnastics scooters and push with their hands on the floor around the designated area (without bumping into one another).

Tightrope Walker. Children walk across a balance beam in several ways (forward, sideways, backward).

Cannonball. Children jump from the top of a small gymnastics box or bench onto a floor mat. While in the air, children make a shape (e.g., C, S, tuck, star) and then land on two feet and hold the landing position for three seconds.

Mule Kicks. Children place both hands on floor mats with arms straight and shoulder-width apart and head looking forward at the floor mat. They kick up their legs toward the ceiling and try to kick out with both feet, like a mule. Mule Kicks are a good progression toward handstands.

Rolly Polly Clown. Children perform various rolls, such as the log roll, shoulder roll, forward roll, or their own created roll, on the mats provided.

Trapeze Artist. Children can either climb the rope to a certain designated height (identified by a ribbon tied to the rope) or hold onto the rope and perform various poses, such as left leg outstretched, right leg outstretched, both legs tucked up, and so on.

Lion Jumps. Place a rope across two small cones to make a hurdle. Use beanbags on top of each cone to keep the rope in position. Have children jump or leap over the ropes five or six times in a row.

Safety Considerations

▷ Ensure that children know how to roll properly and that enough space is allowed between stations. Explain and demonstrate acceptable floor rolls.

▷ Place floor mats next to equipment and in landing areas.

▷ Assist children onto the box top or benches as necessary.

▷ When performing Mule Kicks children should keep their chins well away from their chests, with head looking forward. This helps prevent overbalancing.

Variations

▷ Create new station activities to represent new circus acts such as a Super Skipper Clown and so on.

▷ Mule Kicks can be performed using gymnastics benches to support the hands.

▷ For a cross-curricular approach, use this activity in a social studies unit and discuss circus events in the community.

Assessment

▷ Discuss the importance of strength and overall fitness required to do the circus exercises.

▷ Have children draw their favorite part of the Circus Circuit and identify the major body parts used at each station. Keep drawings in the children's assessment portfolios.

FITNESS MEDLEY

Objectives

To improve bone and muscle strength, muscular endurance, and cardiovascular fitness; to promote jumping, hopping, and leaping skills

Equipment Needed

- ▷ Three hoops
- ▷ Floor mats
- ▷ Four cones
- ▷ Climbing ropes
- ▷ Balance beam or bench
- ▷ Jump ropes
- ▷ Station signs to indicate the name of the activity at each circuit station

Setup

See the diagram for how to organize the stations in this order: Hoop Hopping, Rope Swing, Bench Balance, Curl-Ups, Jumping, Push-Ups, and Jump Rope.

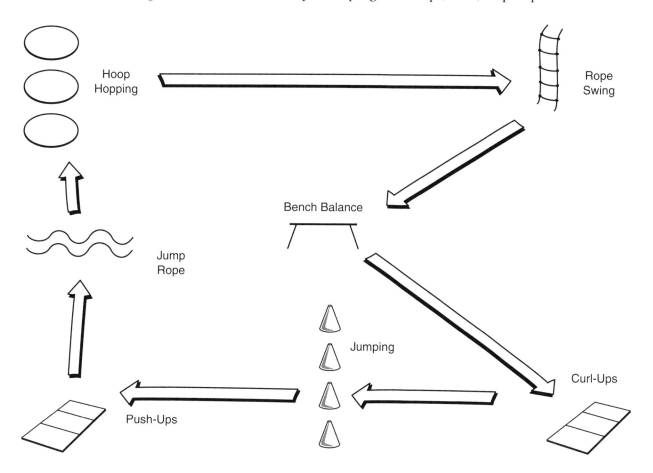

Instructions

Children perform a series of exercises. Each group of children rotates through the stations performing exercise activities at each station for 30 seconds.

Stations

Hoop Hopping. Children hop from hoop to hoop.

Rope Swing. Children hang onto a rope and swing.

Bench Balance. Children walk on a balance bench.

Curl-Ups. Children lie on their backs with feet flat, knees bent, and arms on the floor at their sides, palms down. They raise their bodies about 30 to 45 degrees, then return to the starting position.

Jumping. Children travel in and out and around cones by jumping with feet together.

Push-Ups. Children lie on their bellies with chests touching the floor and feet together. Hands are under the shoulders, palms down. Children push and raise their bodies by extending their arms. They should raise their bodies into a straight line, not allowing their backs to arch. They then lower their bodies back to the floor.

Jump Rope. Children leap over jump ropes stretched on the floor.

Safety Considerations

▷ Allow enough space between stations.

▷ Place hoops close together on the floor.

▷ Place floor mats under climbing ropes and around the balance bench.

▷ Do push-ups and curl-ups on floor mats.

▷ Ensure proper form of exercises and acceptable behavior when waiting at each station.

Variations

▷ With exercise circuits, variations are endless. We suggest setting up stations in a way that ensures that each muscle group gets to rest. For example, after a push-up station, rotate children to a station in which the activity emphasizes lower body muscles.

▷ Increase the amount of time at each station. Ask children to perform a set number of repetitions at each station. Ask children to take turns using alternate feet when hopping and leaping.

Assessment

▷ Observe each child for proper movement form and for cooperative behavior at each station.

▷ Children can work on goal setting by noting their performances in fitness journals or personal activity log books. Keep journals or logs in the child's assessment portfolio.

SIMPLE CIRCUIT

Objectives

To improve bone and muscle strength, agility, movement coordination, and cardio-vascular endurance; to promote jumping skills

Equipment Needed

▷ Cones
▷ Beanbags
▷ Jump ropes
▷ Floor mats
▷ Station signs to indicate the name of the activity at each circuit station

Setup

▷ We recommend organizing your stations in this order, as shown in the diagram: Jogging, Push-Ups, Pick-Ups, Curl-Ups, and Skipping.
▷ Place cones around the perimeter for joggers.

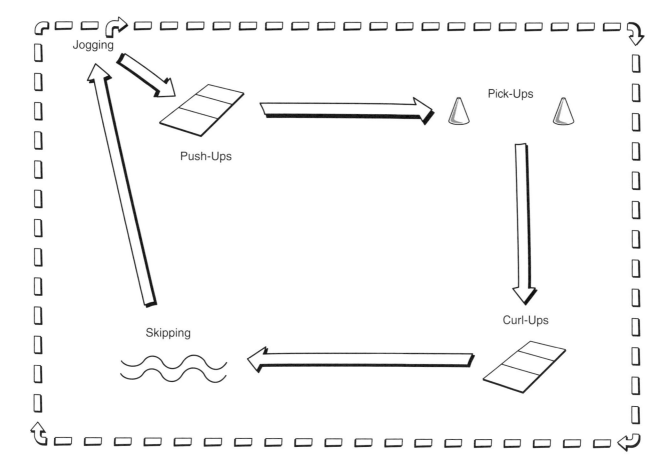

Stations

Jogging. Children jog at an easy pace around the designated cones.

Push-Ups. Children do regular push-ups or modified push-ups either on their knees or standing up against a wall. For modified push-ups on knees, a regular push-up is performed but on the knees instead of the feet. For modified push-ups against the wall, children place their palms against the wall, shoulder-width apart with arms straight. They then bend the elbows to touch their nose to the wall, before pushing back to the straight-arm upright position.

Pick-Ups. Place cones 20 feet (6 meters) apart. Place a beanbag at each cone. Children pick up one beanbag and sprint to the other cone, drop the beanbag and pick up the new beanbag, and sprint back to the cone at which they started. Repeat until it's time to change stations.

Curl-Ups. Children should keep their lower back on the floor at all times during the curl-up.

Skipping. Children either do regular rope jumping or place ropes on the ground and jump back and forth over them.

Safety Considerations

▷ Use mats for curl-up and push-up stations.

▷ Allow enough space for a running track around the other stations.

▷ Always check for proper form of the exercises.

Variations

Ask children to move through each station at their own pace with a set number of repetitions of each exercise, or place a time limit (e.g., 30 seconds) at each station.

Assessment

Children can work on goal setting by noting their performances in fitness journals or personal activity log books. Keep journals or logs in the child's assessment portfolio.

JUMP TO IT!

Objectives

To develop and improve lower body strength, bone development, and aerobic endurance (muscle strength, jumping skills). Although the jumping activities are relatively easy, the cardiovascular workout the children receive is a bonus.

Equipment Needed

▷ Cones
▷ Ropes
▷ Hoops
▷ Floor mats
▷ Beanbags
▷ Chalk
▷ Station signs to indicate the name of the activity at each circuit station

Setup

We recommend organizing your stations in this order, as shown in the diagram: Frog Jumps, One-Foot Jumps, Standing Long Jumps, Hurdle Jumps, and Vertical Jumps.

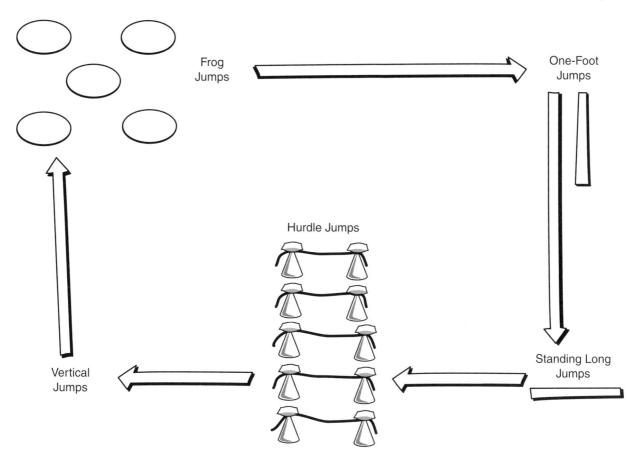

Stations

Frog Jumps. Place hoops on the floor close together to serve as lily pads. Children frog jump to each lily pad.

One-Foot Jumps. Children perform one-foot hops along a straight line painted or taped on the gym floor. They can also hop over the line, moving from side to side. They should change hopping feet after several hops.

Standing Long Jumps. Place a piece of tape or use a line on the floor as a starting line. Children place feet together with toes touching the starting line and then take one jump forward to see how far they can jump and land on both feet. Ensure that children jump from a stationary starting position only—no running starts (because they cause too much forward momentum and make children fall forward on landing). Allow enough time for multiple jumps per child and ask them to record their results and try to improve throughout the year.

Hurdle Jumps. Place a rope across two small cones to form a hurdle. Use beanbags on top of each cone to keep the rope in position. Adjust the height of the rope to accommodate the developmental level of the child performing the jumps. Set up three or four hurdles in a row and have children take two-foot (feet together) jumps over each one.

Vertical Jumps. Children stand facing the wall in a semicrouched position. They jump straight up in the air and touch the wall as high as they can with two hands or one hand before landing on two feet. Children record their marks and work on improving throughout the year. Putting chalk on their fingers before they jump helps them see their marks on the wall.

Safety Considerations

▷ Allow adequate space between stations.

▷ Ensure all exercises are performed correctly.

▷ Use floor mats as necessary.

▷ Make sure shoelaces are tied before children start jumping.

Variations

▷ You can include some push-up or curl-up stations for upper body strength. This provides a mix of upper body and lower body exercises in the station activities.

▷ For a cross-curricular approach, use this activity as part of a science unit on the anatomy of the body. The activity could also relate to math lessons on measuring, recording, and charting.

Assessment

▷ Using the checklist in appendix B, observe and record proper jumping technique at stations.

▷ Ask children to track their progress in their journal or by using goal-setting charts.

MUSCLE-BUILDING CIRCUIT

Objectives

To improve bone and muscle strength and cardiovascular and muscular endurance; to develop jumping, sliding, and balancing skills

Equipment Needed

▷ Cones

▷ Benches or balance beams

▷ Floor mats

▷ Station signs to indicate the name of the activity at each circuit station

Setup

We recommend organizing your stations in this order, as shown in the diagram: Skiers, Modified Push-Ups, Quarter Turns, Tummy Tension, Step or Bench Dips, Jumping Jacks or Janes, and Crab Walk.

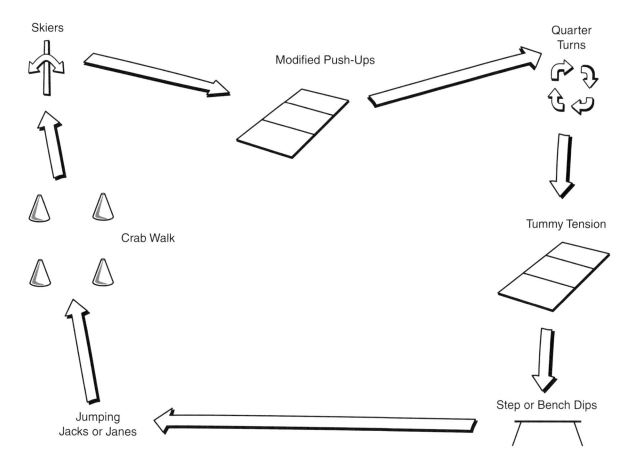

Stations

Skiers. Children jump back and forth over a line with feet together.

Modified Push-Ups. The activity is done on a floor mat. On hands and knees, children lean forward to put their weight on their arms. They slowly bend at the elbows to lower themselves until their nose is just above the floor; they then raise themselves back up by straightening the arms. The back remains straight throughout the movement.

Quarter Turns. Children jump to face all four walls in the area, changing direction after each full turn.

Tummy Tension. This activity is done on a floor mat. Children position themselves with legs stretched out and together. They place their hands on their thighs and lean back slightly, holding for 10 seconds, before sitting back up. They should repeat the exercise several times.

Step or Bench Dips. Children sit with their backs against a low step or bench with their legs together and bent at the knees and feet flat on the floor. Reaching behind and placing their hands firmly on the step or bench, they then push up, using their arms only, to raise their bodies and then slowly lower back down to sitting position. *Modification:* To decrease the difficulty of this exercise, allow children to push with both their feet and arms to raise their hips off the floor. You can also allow children to push with their arms and feet to move their hips upward to finish sitting on the step or bench. To increase the level of difficulty, have children keep their legs together in a straight-leg position with their heels touching the floor.

Jumping Jacks or Janes. Children jump up and down spreading their feet apart, then bringing them back together, while clapping their hands overhead. Hands return to the sides of the body between jumps. *Variation:* Have children extend their arms in an upward direction, straight, and sideways to form a star shape while they jump.

Crab Walk. Children sit upright on the floor and place their hands on the floor behind their hips. They then push up so their bellies are facing the ceiling and their bodies are supported by their hands and feet only. They crab walk forward around a set of cones. After two circles, they change direction. *Variation:* Have children walk backward or sideways, changing their locomotor activity to a gallop, side-step slide, or skip.

Safety Considerations

Allow enough space between stations and make sure all exercises are performed properly, using floor mats when appropriate.

Variations

▷ Ask children to run once around the entire circuit area before moving on to the next station.

▷ For a cross-curricular approach, use this activity as part of a science unit on the anatomy of the body.

Assessment

▷ Ask children to identify and record the muscles and bones they use at each of the stations.

▷ Children can track and report their progress through journal writing or using goal-setting charts.

OLYMPIC EVENTS CIRCUIT

Objectives

To improve bone and muscle strength and jumping and hopping skills; to promote balance, agility, transfer of weight, coordination, flexibility, and muscular and cardiovascular endurance

Equipment Needed

- ▷ Scooters
- ▷ Jump ropes
- ▷ Cones
- ▷ Hoops
- ▷ Floor mats
- ▷ Station signs to indicate the name of the activity at each circuit station

Setup

We recommend organizing your stations in this order, as shown in the diagram: Boxing Rope Skip, Skiing, Skeleton Bobsled, Triple Jump, Gymnastics, and Hockey.

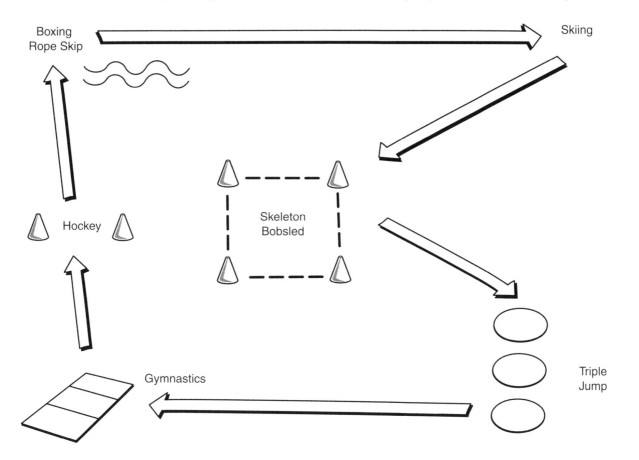

Instructions

Children move through each station performing sets of exercise activities to improve muscular strength and endurance.

Stations

Boxing Rope Skip. Children jump rope on their own, trying different speeds and tricks. They can move forward, backward, sideways, and so on.

Skiing. With their backs flat against a wall, children slide down until their knees are about 90 degrees, at which point they stop and hold position. They maintain the position for as long as they can, then rest and repeat. Ask them to record their times and try to improve them the next time they do this activity.

Skeleton Bobsled. On scooters, children lay on their bellies and move around the perimeter of the Skeleton Bobsled station, using only their arms. Remind them to watch for other bobsleds and children at other stations.

Triple Jump. Using only one leg, children hop through each of the three hoops. When they finish, they turn and hop through the hoops again using the other leg.

Gymnastics. Ask children to create a routine that includes a balancing activity, a jump, and a roll. Have them change the routine each time they visit this station.

Hockey. Place two cones on the floor 20 feet (6 meters) apart. Children perform lunge steps from one cone to the other, then rest and repeat. To perform a lunge, children step forward with the right foot while bending the right knee to a 45-degree angle. They then return to the starting position by bringing the right foot back beside the left foot. They then repeat the sequence using the left leg.

Safety Considerations

▷ Always demonstrate each exercise.

▷ Make sure that children on the scooters stay on the outside of the circuit and that no contact occurs among scooters.

▷ Use floor mats for gymnastics activities.

Variations

▷ Ask children to create different events, such as a sprinting agility run station or a rowing station using resistance bands.

▷ For a cross-curricular approach, include this activity as part of a lesson on the Olympics.

Assessment

▷ Look for proper form during all exercises (see appendix B).

▷ Ask children questions about the events and places in the Olympic Games.

▷ Have children draw their favorite Olympic event or athlete. Store their work in their assessment portfolios.

HEALTHY BONES CIRCUIT TRAINING 1 — *Developmental Level* (2)

Objectives

To improve bone and muscle strength, agility, and balance; to promote running, jumping, and hopping skills and cardiovascular endurance

Equipment Needed

- ▷ Cones
- ▷ Hoops
- ▷ Aerobic steps, small platform, or low bench
- ▷ Floor mats
- ▷ Station signs to indicate the name of the activity at each circuit station

Setup

We recommend organizing your stations in this order, as shown in the diagram: Jumping Jack Flash, Leaping Lizards, Mogul Munchers, Disco Dancers, Terrific Triathletes, Hula Hoppers, Rapid Relay Racers, Speedy Steppers, and Super Stunt Stars.

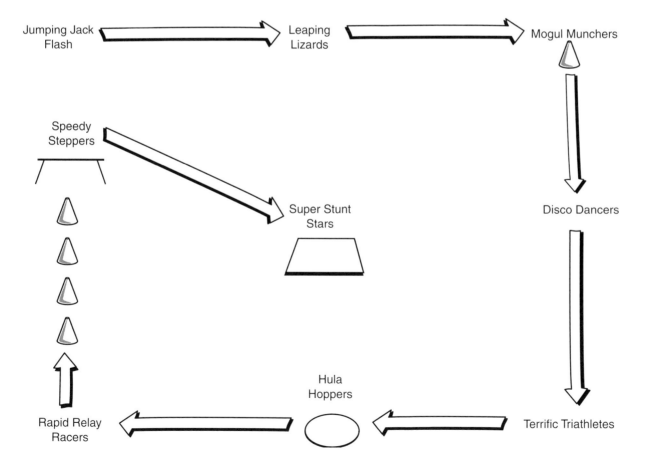

Instructions

Get children to move through a set of stations performing exercises designed to improve bone and leg strength. Activity cards are provided for each of these stations starting on page 22. (Note that this is the first of three Healthy Bones circuits. The other two circuits are explained in the next section under developmental level 3). The length of time spent at each station should gradually progress from 30 to 60 seconds.

Stations

Jumping Jack Flash. Starting with legs together and hands at their sides, children jump, spreading their legs and bringing their arms out to the sides; they then land lightly with knees slightly bent and then jump back to starting position. The motion is repeated to make for continuous movement.

Leaping Lizards. Standing with feet together, children do a small hop to a lunge position, hop again to switch legs, and return to starting position. Repeat the exercise several times.

Mogul Munchers. Standing beside a small cone with feet together, children perform a low jump over the cone, keeping their feet together. They then bounce on both feet and perform a low jump back over the cone. Repeat the exercise several times.

Disco Dancers. Standing with feet shoulder-width apart, children bring one knee up and to the side and bounce on the opposite foot. They then repeat the movement with the opposite knee, alternating legs for a continuous movement activity.

Terrific Triathletes. Standing with feet shoulder-width apart, children run in place. They should do 20 knee-lifts (10 with each leg) before resting and then repeating.

Hula Hoppers. Give each child a hoop. Standing outside the hoop with their feet together, children alternate jumping into the hoop, landing, and then jumping back out of the hoop to the other side in one continuous action.

Rapid Relay Racers. Arrange four cones in a straight line per child. Children start facing the first cone, then skip around each of the four cones in a figure-eight style. After skipping around the fourth cone, they run back to the start and repeat.

Speedy Steppers. Each child stands in front of a step. He or she steps onto the step and then jumps off, landing on the other side. Have children turn and repeat for a continuous movement activity.

Super Stunt Stars. Each child steps onto a step and then jumps off, landing on the other side. Have children turn and repeat, creating different shapes in the air during their jumps.

Safety Considerations

▷ Always demonstrate each exercise. Ensure that children are performing the exercises correctly and that they are jumping at the appropriate height and landing safely.

▷ If children are jumping off a platform, step, or stair, use floor mats for landings.

Variations

▷ Ask children to make up and name their own jump routines.

▷ For a cross-curricular approach, use this activity as part of a science unit on the skeletal system and how to keep bones healthy.

Assessment

▷ Have children record their progress in their activity log books or in their writing journals. Store these in their assessment portfolios.

▷ Discuss the importance of healthy bones. Ask children, "What else makes your bones strong?"

JUMPING JACK FLASH

Equipment

None

Starting Position

- Stand with legs together and hands at side.

Action

- Jump and spread legs (as if doing a jumping jack).
- Bring arms up to shoulder height.
- Land lightly on slightly bent knees.

From *Building Strong Bones & Muscles*, Graham Fishburne, Heather McKay, and Stephen Berg (2005). Champaign, IL: Human Kinetics.

LEAPING LIZARDS

Equipment

None

Starting Position

- Stand with feet together.

Action

- Take a short hop to a lunge position.
- Hop again to switch legs.
- Bounce to return to starting position.

From *Building Strong Bones & Muscles*, Graham Fishburne, Heather McKay, and Stephen Berg (2005). Champaign, IL: Human Kinetics.

MOGUL MUNCHERS

Equipment

One cone per child

Starting Position

- Stand beside cone with feet together.

Action

- Jump over cone with feet together.
- Bounce with feet together.
- Jump over cone with feet together.

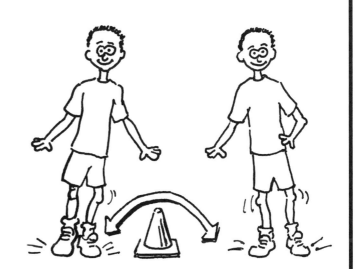

From *Building Strong Bones & Muscles*, Graham Fishburne, Heather McKay, and Stephen Berg (2005). Champaign, IL: Human Kinetics.

DISCO DANCERS

Equipment

None

Starting Position

- Stand with feet shoulder-width apart.

Action

- Bring one knee up to the side.
- Bounce on opposite foot.
- Repeat with other leg up.

From *Building Strong Bones & Muscles*, Graham Fishburne, Heather McKay, and Stephen Berg (2005). Champaign, IL: Human Kinetics.

TERRIFIC TRIATHLETES

Equipment

None

Starting Position

- Stand with feet shoulder-width apart.

Action

- Run on the spot.
- 20 knee-lifts (10 each leg).
- Stand and count to 10.
- Repeat until whistle blows.

From *Building Strong Bones & Muscles*, Graham Fishburne, Heather McKay, and Stephen Berg (2005). Champaign, IL: Human Kinetics.

HULA HOPPERS

Equipment

One hoop per child

Starting Position

- Stand outside the hoop with feet together.

Action

- Jump into the hoop and land.
- Jump out of the hoop to the other side and then back into the hoop again (one continuous action).

From *Building Strong Bones & Muscles*, Graham Fishburne, Heather McKay, and Stephen Berg (2005). Champaign, IL: Human Kinetics.

RAPID RELAY RACERS

Equipment

Four cones per child, arranged in a straight line

Starting Position

- Stand facing first cone.

Action

- Skip around cones in figure-eight style.
- Run back to start.
- Repeat until whistle blows.

From *Building Strong Bones & Muscles*, Graham Fishburne, Heather McKay, and Stephen Berg (2005). Champaign, IL: Human Kinetics.

SPEEDY STEPPERS

Equipment

One step per child

Starting Position

- Stand in front of step.

Action

- Step up onto the step.
- Jump off the step.

From *Building Strong Bones & Muscles*, Graham Fishburne, Heather McKay, and Stephen Berg (2005). Champaign, IL: Human Kinetics.

SUPER STUNT STARS

Equipment

One step per child

Starting Position

- Stand on step.

Action

- Jump off step with own creative movement.

From *Building Strong Bones & Muscles*, Graham Fishburne, Heather McKay, and Stephen Berg (2005). Champaign, IL: Human Kinetics.

HEALTHY BONES CIRCUIT TRAINING 2 — Developmental Level ②③

Objectives

To improve bone and muscle strength, agility, and balance; to promote running, jumping, and hopping skills and cardiovascular endurance

Equipment Needed

- Cones
- Hoops
- Aerobic steps (provide risers if using aerobic steps), small wooden gymnastics box top, platform, or bench
- Floor mats
- Station signs to indicate the name of the activity at each circuit station

Setup

This circuit uses the same station setup as in Healthy Bones Circuit Training 1 described earlier (see diagram).

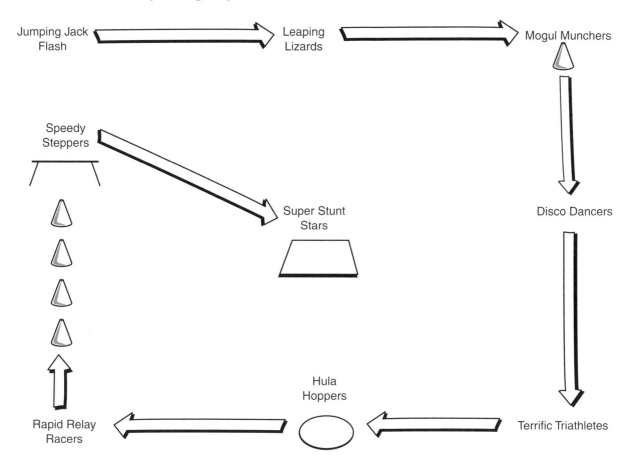

Instructions

Children complete a series of exercises to improve their bone and muscle strength. This is the second of three Healthy Bones circuits. The first circuit was explained under developmental level 2. The second circuit uses the same station activities as the first circuit but with slight adjustments to increase the level of difficulty and work needed to complete the tasks (see activity cards for Healthy Bones Circuit Training 2 on pages 30-34). The length of time spent at each station should gradually progress from 30 to 60 seconds.

Stations

Jumping Jack Flash. Starting with legs together and hands at their sides, children jump and spread their legs while bringing their arms overhead. They land with their legs spread and bent slightly and then jump from bent-leg position to the starting position. They should repeat the sequence for continuous action.

Leaping Lizards. Standing with their feet together, children jump into a lunge position with their legs bent, jump again and change the front foot, and then return to the starting position. They should repeat the sequence for continuous action.

Mogul Munchers. You'll need one small cone per child. Standing beside their cone with their feet together, children do a full jump over the cone, keeping feet together, then do a full jump back to the starting side. They should repeat the sequence for continuous action.

Disco Dancers. Standing with their feet shoulder-width apart, children bring one knee up and to the side; they then bring the knee back down and repeat with the other leg. (This is the same activity as described in Healthy Bones Circuit Training 1, but the bounce is omitted.)

Terrific Triathletes. Standing with feet shoulder-width apart, children hop from side to side, swinging their arms in a skating style.

Hula Hoppers. You'll need one hoop per child. Children stand outside the hoop with their feet together. In one continuous action, they jump into the hoop, land on one foot, then jump back out to the other side. They should repeat the sequence, alternating legs, for continuous action.

Rapid Relay Racers. For each child, you'll need four cones arranged in a line. Children begin standing, facing the first cone. Keeping their feet together, they jump around each cone until they reach the end, and then they run back to the start. They should repeat the sequence for continuous action.

Speedy Steppers. You'll need one step and two risers per child. Each child stands in front of the step, then steps onto it and, with feet together, jumps down to land on the other side. Each child then turns around and repeats the action, jumping onto the side he or she started from. Children should repeat the sequence for continuous action.

Super Stunt Stars. You'll need one step and two risers per child. Each child stands in front of the step, steps onto it, and then jumps off, creating a shape in the air before landing on the other side. Children turn around and repeat the action, landing on the side they started from. Have them repeat the sequence for continuous action, creating different shapes with each jump.

Safety Considerations

▷ Always demonstrate each exercise. Ensure that children are performing the exercises correctly and that they are jumping from appropriate heights.

▷ If children are jumping off a platform, step, or stair, use mats for landings.

Variations

▷ Children can make up and name their own jump routines.

▷ For a cross-curricular approach, use this activity as part of a science unit on the skeletal system and how to keep bones healthy.

Assessment

▷ Use a checklist (appendix B) to assess jumping skills.

▷ Have children record their progress in their activity log books or in their writing journals.

▷ Discuss the importance of healthy bones. Ask children, "What else makes your bones strong?"

JUMPING JACK FLASH

Equipment

None

Starting Position

- Stand with legs together and hands at sides.

Action

- Jump and spread legs.
- Bring arms overhead.
- Land with legs bent.
- Jump from bent-leg position to starting position.

From *Building Strong Bones & Muscles*, Graham Fishburne, Heather McKay, and Stephen Berg (2005). Champaign, IL: Human Kinetics.

LEAPING LIZARDS

Equipment

None

Starting Position

- Stand with feet together.

Action

- Jump to lunge position.
- Jump again to change the front foot.
- Return to starting position.

From *Building Strong Bones & Muscles*, Graham Fishburne, Heather McKay, and Stephen Berg (2005). Champaign, IL: Human Kinetics.

MOGUL MUNCHERS

Equipment

One cone per child

Starting Position

- Stand beside cone with feet together.

Action

- Jump over the cone with feet together.
- Jump back to the other side.

From *Building Strong Bones & Muscles*, Graham Fishburne, Heather McKay, and Stephen Berg (2005). Champaign, IL: Human Kinetics.

DISCO DANCERS

Equipment

None

Starting Position

- Stand with feet shoulder-width apart.

Action

- Bring one knee up and to the side.
- Repeat with the other leg up.

(This is the same activity as described in Healthy Bones Circuit Training 1, but the bounce is omitted.)

From *Building Strong Bones & Muscles*, Graham Fishburne, Heather McKay, and Stephen Berg (2005). Champaign, IL: Human Kinetics.

TERRIFIC TRIATHLETES

Equipment

None

Starting Position

- Stand with feet shoulder-width apart.

Action

- Hop from side to side.
- Swing arms, skating style.

From *Building Strong Bones & Muscles*, Graham Fishburne, Heather McKay, and Stephen Berg (2005). Champaign, IL: Human Kinetics.

HULA HOPPERS

Equipment

One hoop per child

Starting Position

- Stand with feet together on one side of the hoop.

Action

- Jump into the hoop, land on one foot, then jump out to the other side.
- Repeat on the other leg.

From *Building Strong Bones & Muscles*, Graham Fishburne, Heather McKay, and Stephen Berg (2005). Champaign, IL: Human Kinetics.

RAPID RELAY RACERS

Equipment

Four cones per child, arranged in a straight line

Starting Position

- Stand facing first cone with feet together.

Action

- Jump around cones with feet together.
- Run back to start.
- Repeat until whistle blows.

From *Building Strong Bones & Muscles*, Graham Fishburne, Heather McKay, and Stephen Berg (2005). Champaign, IL: Human Kinetics.

SPEEDY STEPPERS

Equipment

One step and two risers per child (one riser under each side of the step)

Starting Position

- Stand facing the step.

Action

- Step up onto the step.
- Jump off.

From *Building Strong Bones & Muscles*, Graham Fishburne, Heather McKay, and Stephen Berg (2005). Champaign, IL: Human Kinetics.

SUPER STUNT STARS

Equipment

One step and two risers per child (one riser under each side of the step)

Starting Position

- Step up onto the step.

Action

- Children create shapes of their own while jumping off the step.

From *Building Strong Bones & Muscles,* Graham Fishburne, Heather McKay, and Stephen Berg (2005). Champaign, IL: Human Kinetics.

HEALTHY BONES CIRCUIT TRAINING 3 — Developmental Level ③

Objectives

To improve bone and muscle strength, agility, and balance; to promote running, jumping, and hopping skills and cardiovascular endurance

Equipment Needed

▷ Cones

▷ Hoops

▷ Aerobic steps (provide risers if using aerobic steps), a small wooden gymnastics box top, platform, or bench

▷ Floor mats

▷ Station signs to indicate the name of the activity at each circuit station

Setup

The circuit uses the same station setup as Healthy Bones Circuit Training 1 and 2 (see diagram).

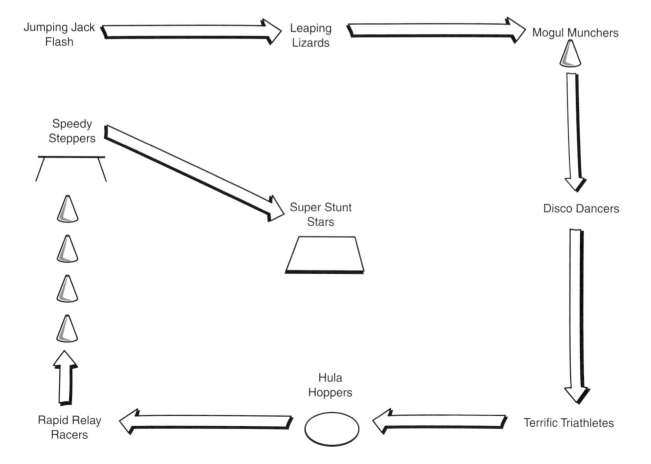

Instructions

Children complete a series of exercises to improve their bone and muscle strength. This is the third of three Healthy Bones circuits. The third circuit uses the same station setup as the first and second circuits, but activities are slightly adjusted to increase the level of difficulty and work needed to complete the tasks (see Activity Cards for Healthy Bones Circuit Training 3 on pages 38-42). Children should complete Healthy Bones Circuit Training 1 and 2 before moving to circuit 3. The length of time spent at each station should gradually progress from 30 to 60 seconds.

Stations

Jumping Jack Flash. Standing with their legs together and hands at their sides, children jump as high as they can. They spread their legs wide to land, while bringing their arms overhead to clap. Have children repeat the sequence for continuous movement action.

Leaping Lizards. Standing with their feet together and hands at their sides, children jump into a tuck position and land in a scissors step with their legs bent. Have them repeat the sequence for a continuous movement action.

Mogul Munchers. You'll need one small cone per child. Children stand beside their cone with their feet together. They then do a Tuck Jump from side to side over their cone.

Disco Dancers. Standing with one leg up, knee bent and slightly to the side, children jump from the leg on the floor to the other leg, trying to get as much height as they can. They should alternate legs, repeating the action in continuous movement.

Terrific Triathletes. Standing with feet shoulder-width apart, children jump from side to side with full power, swinging their arms as if they are skating.

Hula Hoppers. You'll need one hoop per child. Standing outside their hoop with their feet together, children tuck-jump into the hoop and then out of it again to the other side, repeating the exercise for continuous action.

Rapid Relay Racers. You'll need four small cones per child arranged in a straight line. Standing and facing the first cone, children tuck-jump in a straight line over the cones. When they reach the end, they run back to the start and repeat.

Speedy Steppers. You'll need one step and four risers per child. Children stand in front of their step, step onto it, and jump off, landing on the other side. Have them turn and repeat the exercise for continuous action.

Super Stunt Stars. You'll need one step and four risers per child. Children stand in front of the step, step onto it, and jump off, landing on the other side. They then turn and repeat the exercise for continuous action. Have them create different shapes in the air during their jumps.

Safety Considerations

▷ Always demonstrate each exercise. Ensure that children are performing the exercises correctly and that they are jumping at appropriate heights.

▷ If children are jumping off a platform, step, or stair, use floor mats for landings.

Variations

▷ Children can create and name their own jump routines.

▷ For a cross-curricular approach, use this activity as part of a science unit on the skeletal system and keeping bones healthy.

Assessment

▷ Using the checklist in appendix B, assess children's jumping skills.

▷ Have children record their progress in their activity log books or in their writing journals.

▷ Discuss the importance of healthy bones. Ask children, "What else makes your bones strong?"

JUMPING JACK FLASH

Equipment

None

Starting Position

- Stand with legs together and hands at sides.

Action

- Jump up high.
- Spread legs wide to land.
- Bring hands overhead to clap.

From *Building Strong Bones & Muscles*, Graham Fishburne, Heather McKay, and Stephen Berg (2005). Champaign, IL: Human Kinetics.

LEAPING LIZARDS

Equipment

None

Starting Position

- Stand with legs together and hands at sides.

Action

- Jump into a tuck position.
- Land in a scissors step with legs bent.

From *Building Strong Bones & Muscles*, Graham Fishburne, Heather McKay, and Stephen Berg (2005). Champaign, IL: Human Kinetics.

MOGUL MUNCHERS

Equipment

One cone per child

Starting Position

- Stand beside cone with feet together.

Action

- Tuck-jump from side to side over cone.

From *Building Strong Bones & Muscles*, Graham Fishburne, Heather McKay, and Stephen Berg (2005). Champaign, IL: Human Kinetics.

DISCO DANCERS

Equipment

None

Starting Position

- Stand with one leg up and bent.

Action

- Jump from the leg on the floor to the other leg.
- Repeat on initial standing leg.
- Try to get as much height as possible on each jump.

From *Building Strong Bones & Muscles*, Graham Fishburne, Heather McKay, and Stephen Berg (2005). Champaign, IL: Human Kinetics.

TERRIFIC TRIATHLETES

Equipment

None

Starting Position

- Stand with feet shoulder-width apart.

Action

- Jump from side to side with full power.
- Swing arms, skating style.

From *Building Strong Bones & Muscles*, Graham Fishburne, Heather McKay, and Stephen Berg (2005). Champaign, IL: Human Kinetics.

HULA HOPPERS

Equipment

One hoop per child

Starting Position

- Stand on one side of hoop.

Action

- Tuck-jump into the hoop and out again to the other side.

From *Building Strong Bones & Muscles*, Graham Fishburne, Heather McKay, and Stephen Berg (2005). Champaign, IL: Human Kinetics.

RAPID RELAY RACERS

Equipment

Four cones per child, arranged in a straight line

Starting Position

- Stand facing first cone.

Action

- Tuck-jump over cones.
- Run back to start.
- Repeat until whistle is blown.

From *Building Strong Bones & Muscles*, Graham Fishburne, Heather McKay, and Stephen Berg (2005). Champaign, IL: Human Kinetics.

SPEEDY STEPPERS

Equipment

One step and four risers per child (two risers under each side of the step)

Starting Position

- Stand facing the step.

Action

- Step up onto the step.
- Jump off.

From *Building Strong Bones & Muscles*, Graham Fishburne, Heather McKay, and Stephen Berg (2005). Champaign, IL: Human Kinetics.

SUPER STUNT STARS

Equipment

One step and four risers per child (two risers under each side of the step)

Starting Position

- Step up onto the step.

Action

- Children do stunt jumps of their choice off the step.

From *Building Strong Bones & Muscles*, Graham Fishburne, Heather McKay, and Stephen Berg (2005). Champaign, IL: Human Kinetics.

BLASTOFF!

Objectives

To improve bone and muscle strength and cardiovascular endurance; to promote jumping skills

Equipment Needed

▷ Floor mats

▷ Jump ropes

▷ Station signs to indicate the name of the activity at each circuit station

Setup

We recommend organizing your stations as shown in the diagram, placing cones around the perimeter for joggers.

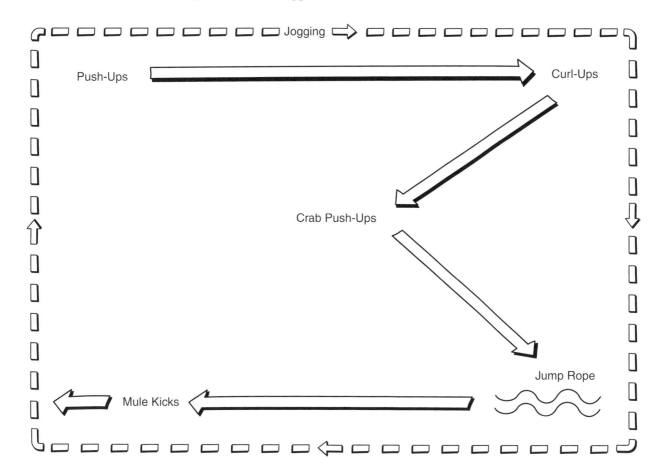

Instructions

Children perform the circuit exercises at each station, gradually increasing their workload. Most of the stations focus on muscular strength, but children will also be doing a lot of jogging to work on their cardiovascular endurance.

Stations

Push-Ups. Children do 1 to 10 push-ups or modified push-ups then jog five laps around the station area.

Curl-Ups. Children do 1 to 10 slow curl-ups then jog four laps around the station area.

Crab Push-Ups. Children do 1 to 10 Crab Push-Ups then jog three laps around the station area.

Jump Rope. Children do 15 to 50 jumps with the jump rope then jog two laps around the station area.

Mule Kicks. Children do 1 to 10 Mule Kicks then jog one lap around the station area.

Safety Considerations

▷ Make sure children go at their own pace or level of fitness.

▷ Watch for proper form of the exercises.

Variations

▷ Children can walk around the perimeter instead of jogging.

▷ Increase or decrease the number of stations or laps that children jog.

Assessment

▷ Have children work on personal goal setting using task cards. Check off goals as they are achieved.

▷ Ask questions about the major muscle groups being worked at each station (e.g., "Besides sit-ups, what else do we need strong abdominal muscles for?").

RESISTANCE TRAINING

Objectives

Resistance training with exercise bands will help children improve muscle fitness. Muscle fitness includes muscle strength, endurance, power, and flexibility.

Equipment Needed

- ▷ Resistance bands or tubes for each child
- ▷ Chairs or benches for children to sit on
- ▷ Station signs to indicate the name of the activity at each station

Setup

None

Instructions

1. At the start of each exercise, have children adjust the length of the band until some resistance is felt (the shorter the band, the greater the resistance). Set resistance levels to correspond with the developmental level of the child.

2. Start with 5 repetitions and gradually build up to 10 over a number of completions of the circuit. However, as with all circuit activities, the number of repetitions can be set on an individual basis to correspond with developmentally appropriate personal goal setting identified on individual task cards.

Stations

Two-Arm Lateral Raise. Children can be seated or standing. Place the exercise band under both feet and ask them to hold one end in each hand, with arms kept at their sides. They then lift arms up and straight out to the side of the body to shoulder level, hold for two seconds, and return to starting position. Begin with 5 repetitions and progress to 10, or set specific numbers of repetitions to correspond with personal goal setting.

Shoulder Shrug. As children are standing, place the exercise band under both feet and ask them to hold one end in each hand. They lift their shoulders a few inches toward their ears, keeping arms straight, hold for two seconds, and return to starting position. Have them do 5 to 10 repetitions or a number that corresponds to their personal goal setting.

Chest Press. Children are seated or standing. Place the exercise band around the upper back and under the arms. Next, grasp both ends of the exercise band with each hand and, while keeping the band taut, have elbows bent at 90 degrees with palms facing down. They then press arms forward until parallel to the ground at shoulder height, hold for two seconds, and return to starting position. Have them do 5 to 10 repetitions or a number that corresponds to their personal goal setting.

Seated Row. Children are in a seated position with legs extended. Place the exercise band around both feet and have them hold one end with each hand. They then pull their arms upward toward the chest until their elbows are at shoulder level, hold for two seconds, and return to starting position. Have them do 5 to 10 repetitions or a number that corresponds to personal goal setting.

Biceps Curl. Children are seated or standing. Place the exercise band under their feet and ask them to hold one end in each hand and keep the band taut. They then curl hands upward toward shoulder height, keeping elbows close to the sides of the body, hold for two seconds, and return to starting position. Have them do 5 to 10 repetitions or a number that corresponds to personal goal setting.

Triceps Extension. As children are standing, place one end of the exercise band in their right hand; their left hand is behind their back, grasping the other end at that point. Ask them to straighten their right arm toward the ceiling, hold for two seconds, and return to starting position. Have them do 5 to 10 repetitions with each arm or a number that corresponds to personal goal setting.

Squat. As children are standing, place the exercise band under their feet and ask them to hold one end in each hand. Keeping their back straight, they bend at the hips, as if they are going to sit in a chair. Ask them to hold for two seconds and then return to starting position. Have them do 5 to 10 repetitions or a number that corresponds to personal goal setting.

Safety Considerations

▷ These routines can be performed in the gym, classroom, or another area large enough for children to exercise.

▷ Replace damaged bands (those with cuts, nicks, and so on).

▷ Make sure there is enough space for each child to perform the exercises.

▷ As with all exercise activities, have children remove all jewelry before using the exercise band.

▷ Exercises should be done in a slow, controlled manner while maintaining good posture (sitting or standing).

▷ Encourage children to breathe normally as they exercise.

Variations

▷ Focus on specific areas of the body for one session or mix them up for a total body workout.

▷ Mix resistance band stations in with other fitness circuits.

▷ For a cross-curricular approach, use this activity as part of a science unit on the skeletal system, force, or keeping muscles healthy.

Assessment

▷ Discuss how resistance training is good for a healthy lifestyle.

▷ Have children record their progress in their activity log books or in their writing journals.

▷ Store feedback in the children's assessment portfolios.

© Human Kinetics

CHAPTER 2

GAME ACTIVITIES

Games and game activities in elementary school physical education develop strength, agility, control, and speed. Games can also improve other areas of physical fitness as well as locomotor skills and sport-specific skills. Games are played throughout the world and usually form the major area covered in school physical education curricula. Because many high-impact and weight-bearing opportunities occur during games play and practice, games and game activities usually promote development of strong bones and muscles.

Developmental Levels

- **Developmental Level 1.** In developmental level 1, game activities emphasize locomotor movements such as running, jumping, hopping, skipping, and galloping. Playing tag, running, and participating in simple team games can promote these skills.

- **Developmental Level 2.** Children in this developmental level still enjoy running and playing tag and simple team games, but you may also introduce children to more organized and challenging games.

- **Developmental Level 3.** Children in this developmental level enjoy more team-oriented sports. However, fitness games such as Popsicle Push-Ups and Boneopoly provide a chance for children to be creative and work cooperatively with other children.

COPY CAT

Objectives

To improve bone and muscle strength; to promote leaping, jumping, hopping, galloping, and skipping skills

Equipment Needed

Flash cards (create one card with the word "Copy" in large letters and another card with the words "Do Not Copy" in large letters)

Setup

Children stand in scattered formation and face the teacher at the front of the room. The teacher has two large flash cards.

Instructions

1. Stand in front of the class with two flash cards. Choose one student to be a leader and ask him or her to stand in front of you to face the rest of the class. The leader begins to perform a movement such as hopping, skipping, jumping, or galloping. The class does not move until you flash one of the two cards.

2. If you flash the Copy card, all children copy the leader's movements. If you flash the Do Not Copy card, children choose their own movement skill to do and do not copy the leader's. The leader performs one movement after another, for about 30 seconds each, as you continue to flash the two cards.

3. Change leaders every three or four movements.

Safety Considerations

Ensure there is enough space for children to move around safely.

Variations

▷ Children (leaders) should be encouraged to perform animal movements, such as the Bear Walk, to develop upper body strength.

▷ For a cross-curricular approach, play Copy Cat in language arts class to practice word recognition. Write action words such as Jump, Hop, or Skip on the flash cards. Children will need to recognize the word and perform the movement action.

Assessment

Observe for listening skills and proper technique of movements.

FROGS AND GRASSHOPPERS

Objectives

To improve bone and muscle strength; to promote jumping and hopping skills

Equipment Needed

Floor mats

Setup

Large circle formation with a floor mat placed beyond the outer edge

Instructions

1. Choose four or five children to be frogs, and the rest are grasshoppers. The frogs sit in the center of a circle formed by the grasshoppers. All children may only hop or jump.
2. Place a mat away from the edge of the circle as a safety zone for the grasshoppers.
3. The grasshoppers hop clockwise in a circle until one of the frogs (or the teacher) claps his or her hands. At the sound of the hand clap, all grasshoppers break from the circle and hop to the safety zone.
4. When grasshoppers are tagged by frogs before reaching the safety zone, they become frogs. A new circle is formed by the remaining grasshoppers, and the game repeats until one grasshopper remains. This player is pronounced the Hopper King (or Queen).

Safety Considerations

▷ Children should tag lightly, without shoving or slapping.
▷ If many children are playing, use more than one safety zone (aim for one safety zone per 8 to 10 children, depending on their size).

Variations

▷ Change motor skills—for example, grasshoppers might skip while frogs gallop.
▷ Use two or three smaller circles to accommodate different levels of ability.
▷ Place safety zone mats closer or further away from the circle to modify the level of difficulty.
▷ For a cross-curricular approach, use animals and insects being covered in the science curriculum.

Assessment

Using the checklists in appendix B, assess proper jumping and hopping techniques.

JUMP THE SNAKE

Objectives

To improve bone and muscle strength and jumping skills; to promote learning of movement concepts

Equipment Needed

Jump rope or another long rope

Setup

Circle formation

Instructions

One player is chosen as Snake Master and stands in the center of a circle formation. This player holds one end of a jump rope (snake) and swings it in a circle about a foot above the ground. The players forming the circle try to jump the snake as it approaches. If touched by the snake, they are charged with a "bite." The game continues for a set time or until a player reaches a designated number of bites. The player with the least number of bites becomes the Snake Master for the next game.

Safety Considerations

▷ Limit the number of players to five or six in each game.

▷ Allow enough space between players forming the circle.

▷ If playing more than one game at a time, allow adequate space between groups.

▷ Monitor the speed and height of the swinging rope to ensure children have success in the activity.

▷ Use jump ropes without heavy hand grips so children cannot be hit by the handles.

Variations

▷ Have children join hands with a partner.

▷ Vary the speed of the rope turn to accommodate the skill level of the players.

▷ For a cross-curricular approach, each time there is a change of Snake Master, ask a math question related to the radius, circumference, or diameter of the circle. For example, if the diameter of the circle is made smaller, what happens to the circumference of the circle? Does it increase or decrease in length?

Assessment

▷ Observe jumping technique.

▷ Have children discuss what a successful jump over the rope looks like (two feet leaving the ground at the same time).

▷ If playing cooperatively with partners, ask children how they were successful in jumping the rope together.

LEAP THE BROOK

Objectives

To promote bone and muscle strength while helping children develop and improve leaping, jumping, galloping, and hopping skills

Equipment Needed

Jump ropes

Setup

Make several "brooks" by placing two jump ropes parallel to each other. Vary the width of each brook (e.g., 24, 36, 42 inches, or 61, 91, 106 centimeters).

Instructions

On signal, children perform locomotor movements such as running, skipping, and galloping. When the teacher calls out, "Leap the brook!" children find a brook and leap or jump over it. They then continue with their locomotor movements until the next call.

Safety Considerations

Only one child at a time should leap over a brook. When two children arrive at one brook, have one leap first, then the other, or ask one to go to a different brook.

Variations

▷ Ask children to perform shapes when jumping over the brook.
▷ Ask them to vary the motor skills they use for traveling and jumping.
▷ For a cross-curricular approach, use this activity with science to discuss the mechanics of body movement.

Assessment

Using the checklists in appendix B, assess proper jumping, galloping, hopping, and leaping techniques.

LEAPING LILY PADS

Objectives

To improve bone and muscle strength; to promote hopping and jumping skills; to help children understand the movement concepts of change in levels and effort

Equipment Needed

Enough mats to cover the gym floor in a line from wall to wall

Setup

Spread a connected band of floor mats across the center of the gym floor, dividing the gym in half. These mats are lily pads for the frogs.

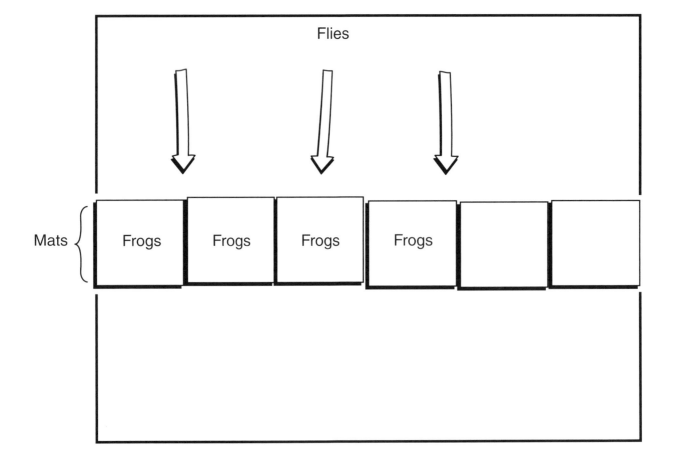

Instructions

Choose at least two children to be frogs; the rest of the children are flies. Designate a starting line 10 to 15 paces in front of the mats on one side of the gym floor. The frogs move along the floor mats in a crouched, hopping manner, while the flies attempt to hop from the starting line across the floor mats to the other side of the gym without being tagged by the frogs. Flies tagged by frogs become frogs. The game continues until one fly remains. Remember to emphasize proper jumping technique. Encourage children to jump as high as they can or to jump for distance within their control.

Safety Considerations

Tagging should be light, with no slapping or shoving.

Variations

- ▷ Change from hopping to two-foot jumping.
- ▷ Move the lily pads around the gym and allow the frogs to jump off their pad to reach a fly.
- ▷ For a cross-curricular approach, use animals and insects being studied in science class.

Assessment

- ▷ Use the checklists in appendix B to assess hopping and jumping skills.
- ▷ Ask children how they can jump higher and farther (crouch low, keep arms behind them, bend at the knees, and so on).

LINE TAG

Objectives

To promote bone and muscle strength while helping children develop and improve their leaping, jumping, hopping, galloping, and skipping skills

Equipment Needed

None

Setup

Use painted or taped lines on the gym floor.

Instructions

1. Using the lines on the gym floor to guide them, children hop, jump, gallop, or skip around the gym.
2. Choose two or three children to be "it." On signal, these children travel along the lines, trying to tag as many children as possible. Limit the children who are "it" to one locomotor skill, such as hopping. When a child is tagged, he or she is now also "it" and joins the tagging group.

Safety Considerations

▷ Discourage children from bumping into each other.
▷ Create a rule for safe movement when children want to pass each other on the same line.

Variations

▷ Play freeze tag. When tagged, children freeze until another child comes along and unfreezes them.
▷ Limit children's movements to certain locomotor skills, such as two-foot jumps.
▷ For a cross-curricular approach, discuss how the body works and the mechanics of movement in a science unit.

Assessment

Using the checklists in appendix B, assess proper technique of locomotor skills.

PUDDLES IN THE SPRING

Developmental Level

Objectives

To improve bone and muscle strength; to promote jumping, running, skipping, and galloping skills; to aid children in learning the movement concepts of relationships and effort

Equipment Needed

One hoop per student

Setup

Scattered formation, each child with a hoop.

Instructions

Children stand behind their puddle (hoop). The teacher then calls out, "In the puddle!" and the children jump into their hoop. The teacher continues to give commands, such as "Jump in," "Jump out," "Behind," and "Around the puddle!" Encourage children to land with both feet at the same time for a bigger "splash."

Safety Considerations

▷ Ensure enough space between hoops.

▷ Tell children not to land on the hoop.

Variations

▷ Have children run, skip, hop, gallop, or side-step around the area until you signal them to jump into their hoops.

▷ Have children jump softly, hard, high, or low into the hoops.

▷ For a cross-curricular approach, ask science questions related to the weather and different seasons. For example, how are puddles formed?

Assessment

▷ Using the checklists in appendix B, assess proper technique of jumping skills.

▷ Ask children how they can jump higher, farther, lower, higher, softer, and so on; have them demonstrate.

ROLL AND JUMP

Objectives

To improve bone and muscle strength; to promote jumping and ball-rolling skills; to aid children in learning the movement concepts of relationships and effort

Equipment Needed

One soft ball for every three children

Setup

Groups of three children in straight lines about 15 feet (4.5 meters) apart.

Instructions

Put children in groups of three, with one child between the other two. The two outside children roll a ball to each other while the child in the middle attempts to jump over the ball. Rotate positions after five attempts.

Safety Considerations

Make sure the ball is always rolled, not thrown.

Variations

▷ Emphasize slow-rolling balls to give children time to prepare and execute their jumps.

▷ Varying the size of the ball changes the level of difficulty. Individual differences in development can be accommodated with slower or faster rolls and smaller or larger balls.

▷ Children can attempt turns or other stunts or shapes in the air as they jump over the ball.

▷ Use small balls rolled slowly to accommodate children with lower levels of motor development.

▷ For a cross-curricular approach, discuss the science concepts of force and the mechanics of human movement.

Assessment

Observe jumping technique and watch for cooperative behavior among children.

ALPHABET RECOGNITION

Objectives

To improve bone and muscle strength; to promote jumping and hopping skills; to aid children in learning the concept of transfer of weight

Equipment Needed

Chalk (if using a blacktop surface)

Setup

Any floor surface area

```
        | Z |
| Y | P | G | O |
| F | X | R | C |
| L | J | T | N |
| S | Q | B | H |
| W | E | M | D |
| K | I | V | U |
        | A |
```

Instructions

Draw several copies of the pattern shown (see diagram) on a blacktop or other floor surface. The size of each square depends on the age or developmental level of the children. Divide children up among the patterns. Player 1 at each pattern begins in square A and attempts to move through the pattern following the alphabet by hopping through the squares, without touching any lines, and landing on all the alphabet letters until finishing on Z. If a child touches a line, he or she must return to letter A to start again. To avoid long lines of children waiting to take their turn, once player 1 has moved through two or three squares, player 2 can start, followed by player 3, and so on. On reaching the letter Z, players start again at letter A, only this time they hop on their other foot. The third time through, two-foot jumping replaces hopping.

Safety Considerations

Ensure adequate space for each group in the playing area.

Variations

For a cross-curricular approach, consider the following possibilities:

▷ Give children task cards with words written on them and have them spell out the words (or they can try to spell each other's names).

▷ Use words from units in social studies, health, science, and so on.

▷ Use numbers in the grid pattern instead of letters and pose challenges involving adding, subtracting, and so on.

Assessment

This activity can be a good way to review or test weekly spelling words or math problems.

CHINESE JUMP ROPE

Objectives

To improve bone and muscle strength; to promote jumping skills and changing direction; to help children learn the movement concept of effort

Equipment Needed

Resistance bands or long elastic ropes (or pantyhose tied in long strips)

Setup

An open area

Instructions

Players 1 and 2 hold a resistance band or elastic rope with their legs at ankle level. Player 3 jumps in various ways inside the resistance band, in and out of the band, or on the band. Player 1 then trades places with player 3 and copies the movements of player 3. If player 1 makes a mistake in copying the movements, he or she trades places with player 2. If successful in copying all the movements of player 3, player 1 then creates his or her own routine, which player 2 tries to copy. Make sure each player has a turn creating movements.

Safety Considerations

Ensure children are jumping safely without exceeding their level of ability.

© Human Kinetics

Variations

▷ Have children raise the height of the resistance band or change positions of their feet to make the sides of the band closer together or wider apart.

▷ Ask children holding the resistance band to pose challenges for the jumper.

▷ For a cross-curricular approach, link the Chinese Jump Rope activity to social studies and discuss cultures, customs, and traditions of China. You can also incorporate counting, adding, and subtracting into the jumping activity.

Assessment

▷ Observe for correct jumping technique.

▷ Ask children to make a chart listing the similarities and differences in Chinese jump rope and regular rope jumping.

CIRCLE TAG

Objectives

To improve bone and muscle strength; to promote pushing and pulling skills; to aid children in learning the concept of change of direction

Equipment Needed

None

Setup

Place children in groups of 8 to 10. Each group forms a circle by holding hands with the other members in their group, except for one player, who is chosen to be "it." The player designated as "it" stands in the middle of the circle.

Instructions

Without breaking hands, the circle players try to touch the player who is "it." Once a player touches the one who is "it," he or she moves into the center of the circle, and the game starts up again.

Safety Considerations

Provide adequate space for children to move.

Variations

▷ Restrict children in the circle to hops or jumps.

▷ For a cross-curricular approach, discuss science concepts related to the mechanics of movement and force.

Assessment

▷ Using the checklists in appendix B, assess proper technique of jumping skills.

▷ Watch for cooperative behavior.

CRAB SOCCER

Objectives

To improve bone strength, muscle strength, kicking, passing, balance, and change of direction; to help children learn the movement concepts of spatial awareness and effort

Equipment Needed

> Cones
> Size 3 or 4 soccer balls

Setup

Using cones for boundaries, set up small playing areas with goals (two cones) at either end.

Instructions

Divide the class up among the playing areas into two teams for each area so that multiple games are playing at once. Players from both teams start in a Crab Walk position and move anywhere in their playing area. Players must move the ball with their feet only, except for the two goalies, who can use their hands as well. The object is to score goals against the opposing team. A foul occurs if a regular player uses his or her hands or kicks the ball out of the playing area. After a foul, give the ball to the nearest player on the team who did not commit the foul.

Safety Considerations

> Have children practice the Crab Walk first.
> Use a foam ball or a beach ball to maximize safety.

Variations

> Use more than one ball during a game.
> Have two goals for each team to defend.
> Let children use hands and feet to strike the ball.
> For a cross-curricular approach, discuss marine life, beginning with crabs, and pose questions about the mechanics of human movement and the movement of crabs.

Assessment

Observe for teamwork and strategy.

GUESS WHAT!

Objectives

To improve bone and muscle strength and overall body coordination; to promote jumping, running, skipping, leaping, galloping, and hopping skills

Equipment Needed

Chalk or tape

Setup

In an open area, draw or tape two lines about 30 to 40 feet (9 to 12 meters) apart; place one player, designated as "it," on one line and the rest of the class on the other line.

Instructions

The group on the line decides on an action word, such as hopping or jumping, and all children copy this movement and move toward "it." As soon as "it" guesses the action correctly, he or she tries to tag everybody before they cross the line. If caught, the players also become "it," and the game continues.

Safety Considerations

Make sure all children have enough space to move.

Variations

▷ Have the children work in groups of three or four.

▷ For a cross-curricular approach, use flash cards to practice word recognition. Hold up a flash card with an action printed on it, such as two-foot jump. Children on the line try to recognize the words and perform the action.

Assessment

Using the checklists in appendix B, assess correct skill development.

LOOSE CABOOSE

Objectives

To improve bone and muscle strength; to promote skills in jumping, running, skipping, leaping, galloping, hopping, dodging, change of direction, and speed; to help children develop and improve their locomotor and agility skills in a cooperative setting

Equipment Needed

None

Setup

An open area

Instructions

1. Choose two players to be loose cabooses and put the remaining children into groups of three. Each group forms a line. The members of each group hold the waist of the person in front of them. The first player is the engine, the second the baggage car, and the third the caboose.

2. On signal, each train moves about the gym in one movement, such as galloping or hopping, and tries to prevent the loose cabooses from attaching to its own caboose. When a loose caboose does attach, the engine is released from the train and becomes a new loose caboose, and each player moves up one place on the train. Loose cabooses are limited to particular movements, such as jumping or skipping.

3. If a train pulls apart at any time, the whole group is considered derailed and must do 10 jumping jacks or tuck jumps before rejoining the game.

Safety Considerations

Allow enough space for children to move around safely.

Variations

▷ Change locomotor movements frequently for trains and loose cabooses.

▷ Increase the group size to form longer trains.

▷ For a cross-curricular approach, discuss trains in science (locomotive, locomotor skills) or social studies (transport).

Assessment

▷ Using the checklists in appendix B, assess correct skill development.

▷ Watch for cooperative behavior.

PARTNER RELAYS

Objectives

To improve bone and muscle strength; to promote hopping and jumping skills

Equipment Needed

Cones

Setup

An open area

Instructions

1. Group children into teams of four or six (even numbers are best.) Have each team divide themselves up into pairs. Each pair stands side by side, holding each other around the waist with their inside arm. One pair lines up at the starting line. On a signal, the pairs hop or jump to the end of the gym, or to a designated cone, and back, tagging the next group on their team to begin their turn.

2. As an extra challenge, and for variety, a bean-bag or ball is held between the pairs as they travel across the gym.

Safety Considerations

▷ Allow enough space for children to move safely.

▷ Relay activities can become quite competitive; some children might value winning over cooperation and correct movement form. If this happens, make changes to reduce the competitive nature. For example, give each group a different movement activity, so that groups will finish the relays at various times because of their different movement requirements. Or put a different number of pairs of children in each group. Again, groups will finish at varied times because the numbers of pairs completing the tasks are not the same.

Variations

▷ Emphasize proper hopping technique so children do not trip and pull each other over.

▷ For a cross-curricular approach, discuss the mechanics of human movement and force.

Assessment

Observe for cooperative behavior.

TRIANGLE TAG

Objectives

To improve bone and muscle strength; to promote sliding and dodging skills, agility, balance, cooperation, and making changes in direction; to help children learn the movement concept of effort

Equipment Needed

None

Setup

An open area

Instructions

Create groups of four players. Three children hold hands, forming a triangle, and the fourth child is "it." One child in the triangle is designated as the one who has to be caught. The child who is "it" runs around the triangle, trying to tag the designated player (but is not allowed to reach across the triangle). The children in the triangle move around and work together to try to save the designated player from being caught. Change roles every 20 to 30 seconds so everyone gets a turn to be "it" and the one to be caught.

Safety Considerations

Allow enough space for each group in the playing area.

Variations

▷ Instead of using only triangle shapes, add more people to form a square, circle, rectangle, or other shapes.

▷ Restrict movements to step-hopping, skipping, two-foot jumping, or another movement.

▷ For a cross-curricular approach, use geometric shapes discussed in math to determine the shapes for the game.

Assessment

Have children write down or discuss all the skills they have learned from this game (e.g., dodging, agility, cooperation, communication).

BONEOPOLY

Objectives

To improve bone and muscle strength and muscular and cardiovascular endurance; to promote jumping, galloping, skipping, hopping, and pushing skills; to help children practice making changes in direction and applying the movement concept of effort

Equipment Needed

▷ Pieces of paper or cardboard for the game board (shown here), dice, markers, cards. If possible, laminate the game board for protection.

▷ Jump ropes

Setup

An open area

Rest	Jump Rope 2 min	Seal Crawl 30 feet	Water	One-Foot Jumps across gym	25 Curl-Ups	Rest
Ski Jump over line 20 X						Wall Sit 30 secs
10 Push-Ups		Muscle	BONEOPOLY!			Teddy Bear Stand
Water						Water
Jog around gym 5 times				Bone		Crab Walk 30 feet
10 Vertical Jumps						1 min Leaping Lizards
Rest	15 Tuck Jumps	25 Curl-Ups	30 Jumping Jacks	10 Push-Ups	Jump Rope 2 min	Rest

Instructions

Boneopoly is similar to the board game Monopoly but with a fitness focus. The idea is to create a game for children to play that will promote muscle and bone development. The teacher can create the game board or can brainstorm with the class to come up with several different boards for children to use. Individuals or small groups roll the dice and perform the activity in the square in which their game piece lands. In the place of community chest and chance cards, have questions for children to answer related to muscle and bone development. For example: Drinking soda weakens bones—true or false? Such questions increase their knowledge of healthy bones and muscles and also serve as rest stations for the children. Be sure to add some water spaces onto the game boards.

Safety Considerations

▷ Make sure children properly warm up and stretch before the game.

▷ Be sure that each activity is developmentally appropriate for the children.

▷ If any activities seem too difficult, change the activity or intensity.

Variations

▷ Put different questions or activities in each square.

▷ Many opportunities present themselves for cross-curricular approaches using Boneopoly. Health and wellness choices can be linked to the items on the game board and the health curriculum, for example.

Assessment

▷ Observe skill development.

▷ Check for increasing knowledge about bones and muscles.

COOPERATIVE JUMPS

Objectives

To improve bone and muscle strength; to promote jumping skills and cooperation

Equipment Needed

Floor tape to identify start and finish lines

Setup

An open area

Instructions

Teams of three to five children start at one end of the gym. Mark starting lines and finish lines with tape on the floor. Start with a distance of 30 feet (about 9 meters). Adjust this distance as necessary to meet the developmental levels of the children. On a signal, the first players on each team perform a standing long jump, land, and remain where they are. The next player does a standing long jump from where the first player is standing. The third player jumps from where the second player lands, and so on. The activity continues until the finish line is reached.

This game can be competitive between teams, or you can have each team estimate how many jumps it will take to reach the finish line. Record scores and have them try to improve on them, or choose a new distance.

Safety Considerations

▷ Allow enough space for all children to jump safely.

▷ Make sure only standing long jumps are performed—no running starts.

Variations

▷ Have children take off on one foot and land on both feet.

▷ Mark off different distances for each team, depending on the developmental levels of the children. Because the distances vary among teams, competition is reduced.

▷ For a cross-curricular approach, use estimation and counting to try to arrive at the number of jumps, hops, and so on required by each team to travel the distances between the lines.

Assessment

Using the checklists in appendix B, assess correct skill development.

FITNESS STICKS

Objectives

To improve bone and muscle strength, cardiovascular endurance, balance, and agility; to promote hopping, jumping, galloping, skipping, and sliding skills; to help children practice transfer of weight and change of direction and to understand the movement concepts of effort and spatial awareness

Equipment Needed

▷ Enough Popsicle sticks for the entire class

▷ Jump ropes

Setup

An open area

Instructions

On Popsicle sticks ("fitness sticks"), write questions or actions involving bone and muscle development. Here are some possibilities:

▷ Walk on your hands and feet across the gym.

▷ Do 10 Tuck Jumps.

▷ Do 5 push-ups, rest, and do 5 more.

▷ What is osteoporosis?

▷ Name 3 bones in the lower body.

▷ Name 3 bones in the upper body.

▷ List 5 foods good for building strong bones.

▷ Do 10 lunges.

▷ Jump rope for 5 minutes.

▷ Do 10 curl-ups.

▷ Do 25 jumping jacks.

▷ Do 10 Frog Jumps.

▷ Does watching television help build muscle? Why not?

▷ Hop on one foot across the gym. Return hopping on the other foot.

▷ Seal Crawl for 30 seconds.

▷ Wall sit for 30 seconds.

▷ Perform the Coffee Grinder both ways.

▷ Name 5 weight-bearing activities.

▷ Jump in the air and perform a stunt.

▷ Do two-foot jumps across the gym.

Each child is given a fitness stick at the beginning of class. The teacher calls out a child's name, and the child reads his or her stick. If the stick is a knowledge question, have students pair up to discuss and answer the question. If an activity is required, the entire class performs the activity.

Safety Considerations

If children perform fitness stick activities without a demonstration, make sure everyone understands the activity and can perform it safely. As necessary, demonstrate the correct movement actions before children do the activity.

Variations

▷ Have children create their own fitness sticks in class, but make sure the activities they choose are safe and developmentally appropriate.

▷ For a cross-curricular approach, discuss the fitness stick questions during health class.

Assessment

Fitness sticks can be a good way to review muscle- and bone-building activities, healthy lifestyle habits, and the benefits of fitness.

Objectives

To improve bone and muscle strength; to promote jumping skills and cooperation

Equipment Needed

Long rope

Setup

An open area

Instructions

Three to nine players stand beside a long jump rope. On a signal, the rope turners begin, and all players jump rope.

© Human Kinetics

Safety Considerations

Allow enough space for all children to jump safely.

Variations

▷ At the start, have jumpers enter one by one. Then have jumpers enter two at a time.

▷ Have jumpers turn in the air as they make their jumps.

▷ For a cross-curricular approach, use this activity to discuss cardiovascular fitness in health class.

Assessment

Observe cooperative skills and jumping form.

OPEN THE WINDOW

Objectives

To improve bone and muscle strength; to promote change of direction and speed and jumping, hopping, running, galloping, and skipping skills

Equipment Needed

None

Setup

Arrange the class into groups of seven. Three sets of partners line up behind a starting line. The other player is the "window" and stands about 10 feet (3 meters) in front of the three sets of partners, facing away from the group.

Instructions

At the beginning, the group of seven decide what locomotor skill will be performed (jump, skip, hop, or gallop). All players, including the window player, must perform the specified locomotor movement. When the window player calls out "Open the window!" the two players (partners) at the back of the line move, one to each side of the line. They then perform the selected motor skill and jump, skip, hop, or gallop up each side of the line and in front of (around) the window player. They must try to pass the window and join up with their partner again without being tagged by the window. Remember that the window player can tag the two players only while using the same locomotor skill. The first player tagged becomes the new window player. The game continues, with all players taking turns to pass the window.

Safety Considerations

▷ Allow enough space for all groups to perform the activity safely.

▷ To make this game cooperative, replace the window player with a cone. Tagging is removed from the game, and players can travel around the cone to meet up with their partner without having to avoid being tagged. The speed of traveling is now determined by each player and not influenced by the moving window.

Variations

▷ Make up new movements such as bear walking for the players to use.

▷ If the window position is not changing regularly during the game, have children take turns being the window.

▷ For a cross-curricular approach, use this activity to discuss the mechanics of human movement and the concept of force in science.

Assessment

Using the checklists in appendix B, assess proper skill development.

POPSICLE PUSH-UPS

Objectives

To improve balance and bone and muscle strength; to promote cooperation

Equipment Needed

Floor mats

Setup

An open area with floor mats spread around.

Instructions

Divide children into groups of four. Working on floor mats, one child lies facedown on the mat, ready to do a push-up. The second child lies at a right angle to the first with the tops of his or her feet on top of the first child's lower back (ready to do a push-up). The third child repeats this action, using the second child's lower back as a footrest. The fourth child does the same, using the third child for a footrest. On a signal, all four in the group attempt to do a push-up. If children have difficulty, have them start their push-up slightly before the rest of the group.

Safety Considerations

Be sure to use floor mats for a softer surface.

Variations

> Have students set goals for how many group push-ups they will do.

> For a cross-curricular approach, the difference between a full push-up and a modified push-up can be discussed in science to determine why a modified push-up is easier to perform.

Assessment

Observe for cooperative behavior, leadership, and positive social skills.

TUG OF PEACE

Objectives

To improve bone and muscle strength and balance; to promote cooperation

Equipment Needed

▷ Strong rope, such as a gymnastics climbing rope

▷ Floor mats

Setup

An open area. Connect floor mats to form a line of attached mats. Place the rope along the line of mats in the center.

Instructions

Begin with class members standing on the mats or floor equal distances apart along the side of a rope. Children count off in 2s, then turn and face each other, so 1s and 2s are facing each other along the length of the rope. On a signal, the 1s pull against the 2s. There is usually no winner.

Safety Considerations

▷ Make sure the rope is strong and in good condition.

▷ Remind children that someone can get hurt if one team lets go of the rope just to see the other team fall.

▷ Check children's footwear for good traction.

Variations

▷ Have children sit on their bottoms. On a signal, each person pulls on the rope to stand up. Exercise caution due to potential falling hazards.

▷ For a cross-curricular approach, use this activity to discuss Newton's law related to action and reaction in science.

Assessment

Observe the class for fair play and cooperative skills.

TUG OF WAR

Objectives

To improve bone and muscle strength and balance; to promote cooperation

Equipment Needed

▷ Strong rope, such as a gymnastics climbing rope
▷ Floor mats

Setup

In an open area, connect floor mats to form a line of attached mats. Place the rope along the line of mats in the center.

Instructions

Divide the class into two relatively equal teams based on the strength and weight of the children. If you have a large class, make four teams. Standing on the floor mats, children have a tug-of-war rope across a centerline and a marker is placed on each side of the rope about 5 to 6 feet (1.5 to 2 meters) from the centerline. On command, each team tries to pull the other team's marker over the centerline.

Safety Considerations

▷ Make sure the rope is in good condition and not frayed.
▷ Remind children that someone can get hurt if one team lets go of the rope just to see the other team fall.
▷ Check children's footwear for good traction.

Variations

▷ Have children sit on their bottoms or face the opposite direction.
▷ For a cross-curricular approach, use this activity to discuss the concepts of inertia and force in science.

Assessment

Observe the class for fair play, teamwork, and cooperative skills.

CHAPTER 3

INSTRUCTIONAL GYMNASTICS ACTIVITIES

Gymnastics activities involve weight bearing, making them effective for improving bone and muscular development. Gymnastics activities for elementary school-aged children can involve locomotor, nonlocomotor, and manipulative skills as well as strength, flexibility, agility, and balance activities. Children move in a safe manner as they learn to move with control and grace. This chapter's activities, which can be performed individually, with partners, or in small groups, are separated into three categories: agility, balance, and rope climbing. The activities are presented in a developmentally and sequentially appropriate manner. If a child has difficulty performing activities in, for example, developmental level 3, either modify the activities (with safety in mind) or have the child perform the easier lead-up activities in developmental levels 1 or 2.

Developmental Levels

- **Developmental Level 1.** In this level, children enjoy simple animal movements, balances, and partner activities. The activities serve as a foundation for more advanced skills in the later developmental stages.

- **Developmental Level 2.** At this level, activities become increasingly more difficult. There should also be a greater emphasis on the quality of the movements. Children at this developmental level enjoy activities with partners and in small groups.

- **Developmental Level 3.** In level 3, children continue to refine the skills they learned in level 2. More strength, power, and control are needed in this level as skills become more advanced.

AGILE ACTIVITIES

Objectives

To improve bone and muscle strength; to promote jumping skills; to help children learn the movement concepts of transfer of weight, change of direction, and effort

Equipment Needed

▷ A floor mat for each child or enough for two children to share

▷ Station signs to indicate the name of the activity at each station

Setup

Gym or open area. If working with a whole group of children, place mats in scattered formation all about the gym floor. If working with small groups of children, create five station areas identified by station signs. Place mats at the station locations.

Instructions

The activities presented in this chapter are designed to help children develop strength and agility. Activities include simple exercises that can be performed individually. These exercises promote bone and muscle development throughout the body. With this in mind, remember to give children frequent rest breaks. These skills can be performed as an entire class or in stations.

Bouncing Ball. Standing with arms and feet shoulder-width apart, children lower their bodies gradually using small jumps until their hands touch the ground. Have them repeat the action upward until back in starting position. *Variation:* Turn the body around as if jumping.

Tuck Jump. Standing with feet shoulder-width apart, knees slightly bent, and arms raised forward and sideways, children jump into the air, pulling their knees up to their chest and wrapping their hands around their lower legs. In the air, they release their grip and land on their toes with knees bent. *Variations:* Jump up and make a straddled leg position (legs straight and wide apart); jump up and touch different parts of the body, calling the body part by name while in the air.

Jump Turns. With knees slightly bent, feet 12 inches (30 centimeters) apart, and arms close to the body, children jump straight up, make a half turn, and land with bent knees. *Variations:* Make a three-quarter or full turn; jump, turn, and clap hands; jump and make a shape in the air during the turn.

One-Foot Jump. Standing on one leg with arms extended forward, children swing their raised leg backward and forward, pushing off the toes in a forward direction. *Variation:* Change legs.

Prone Knee Fall. On their knees on a floor mat, body erect, children fall forward and land on their hands, gradually bending their arms to absorb the fall.

Safety Considerations

▷ Children should take turns when sharing mats.

▷ Allow for individual progression of the movements.

▷ Make sure activities that involve falling or dropping, such as the Prone Knee Fall, are done on floor mats.

Variations

▷ See descriptions of individual activities for possible variations.

▷ For a cross-curricular approach, refer to these activities in science class as practical examples of movements to discuss force, motion, and the mechanics of movement.

Assessment

▷ Using the checklists in appendix B, assess proper skill development.

▷ When children are performing variations, observe for creativity and imagination.

AGILE ANIMALS

Objectives

To improve bone and muscle strength and jumping skills; to promote learning of the following concepts: transfer of weight, change of direction, relationships, and effort

Equipment Needed

▷ A floor mat for each child or enough for two to share

▷ Station signs to indicate the name of the activity at each station

Setup

Gym or an open area. If working with a whole group of children, scatter mats all about the gym floor. If working with small groups, create five station areas identified by station signs. Place mats at the station locations.

Instructions

Agility skills at developmental level 1 include simple animal walks and simple partner activities. These activities promote bone and muscle development of the entire body. With this in mind, be sure to give children frequent rest breaks. These agility skills can be performed by an entire class at once or in stations.

Dog Walk. Beginning in a crouched position, with weight on hands and feet, children move on all fours, keeping their head up. Ask children to move forward, backward, sideways, and so on.

Lame Puppy Walk. As a variation of the Dog Walk, children keep both hands and *one* leg on the floor, keeping their head up while they walk or run in different directions on three "legs." *Variation:* Challenge children to try moving with only one hand and one foot on the floor.

Frog Jump. In a squatting position with their hands on the floor, children jump forward and land on the hands first, then the toes. *Variation:* Try to get children to increase their height and distance.

Leap Frog. One partner squats down while the other stands semi-crouched behind, with legs spread apart and hands raised, as if ready to be placed on the shoulders of the crouching partner. The standing partner then leaps over the squatting partner. *Variation:* Make the activity more challenging by adjusting the height of the crouched partner or adding more children to leap over.

© Human Kinetics

Crab Walk. With their hands and feet on the floor and their bellies facing the ceiling or sky, children walk backward and sideways, trying to keep their seat from touching the floor. *Variation:* Challenge children to balance a beanbag on their belly or forehead.

Safety Considerations

▷ Children should take turns when sharing mats.

▷ Allow for individual progression of the movements.

Variations

▷ See descriptions of individual activities for possible variations.

▷ For a cross-curricular approach, use these activities in science when discussing animals and how different animals move.

Assessment

▷ Using the checklists in appendix B, assess correct skill development.

▷ When children are performing variations, observe for creativity and imagination.

▷ Have children draw their favorite animal.

CARRYING YOUR WEIGHT

Objectives

To improve bone and muscle strength; to improve balance; to promote learning of the concept of weight transfer

Equipment Needed

▷ A floor mat for each child or enough for two to share

▷ Station signs to indicate the name of the activity at each station

Setup

Gym or an open area. If working with a whole group of children, scatter mats all about the gym floor. If working with small groups of children, create four station areas identified by station signs. Place mats at the station locations.

Instructions

Children at developmental level 1 should be performing simple movements that transfer weight from one body part to another. These movements prepare children for more advanced skills in developmental levels 2 and 3. Children will become tired, so allow for frequent breaks. All four activities should be done on floor mats.

Single Mule Kick. In a standing position, raising arms overhead and facing the mat with one foot slightly in front of the other, children bend forward, placing their hands on the mat and kicking their back leg upward.

Mule Kick. In a semicrouched position, with hands shoulder-width apart, knees bent, and feet together, children use one move to place weight on their hands and drive their legs up and back.

Half Cartwheel. With the right or left foot slightly ahead of the other and with arms overhead, children bend forward toward the side of their lead foot. They place their lead hand on the mat or floor, followed by the other, swing around, and land in a partially crouched position. *Variation:* Perform a full cartwheel and finish standing. The back should remain straight throughout the movement.

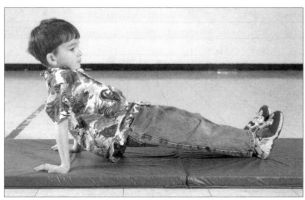

Rear Support. In a seated position, children place their hands flat on the mat next to their body and gradually raise their seat off the mat. They walk legs out until their body is in a straight line. *Variation:* Turn to a front support or balance on one foot and then the other.

Safety Considerations

▷ If necessary, have an adult spotter for the cartwheels.
▷ Allow for individual progression of the movements.

Variations

▷ See descriptions of individual activities for possible variations.
▷ For a cross-curricular approach, use these activities in science when discussing animal movements and the concepts of force and strength.

Assessment

▷ Using the checklists in appendix B, assess correct skill development.
▷ Ask children to identify the parts of the body they use when doing mule kicks.

JUNGLE VINES

Objectives

To improve bone and muscle strength; to help children learn the movement concepts of weight transfer, change of direction, levels, and shapes

Equipment Needed

▷ Floor mats
▷ Climbing ropes

Setup

Place floor mats beneath climbing ropes.

Instructions

Rope work involves climbing, swinging, and movement skills that children at all developmental stages can enjoy. Rope work is beneficial in strengthening arm and shoulder muscles. It is important to allow children to progress at their own level when performing rope skills.

Pull-Ups. Lying on a mat beneath the rope, children hold the rope with both hands and slowly raise their body upward, trying to keep as straight as possible.

Reach and Pull. In a seated position on the mat, children hold the rope overhead and pull their body up, trying to keep their legs extended and parallel to the floor.

Photo courtesy Graham Fishburne

Letter Recognition. Children hang between two ropes and make the shapes of letters with their bodies and limbs. *Variations:* Have other children try to guess what the letters are. Or have a partner call out a letter that the hanging partner tries to shape his or her body into.

Back Roll. Lying with their backs on a mat, children grab a rope with two hands, their arms extended; they pull up on the rope for support and perform a backward roll. *Variation:* During the backward roll, move legs into a tuck or straddle or another position.

Safety Considerations

▷ Children should warm up and stretch their arm and shoulder muscles before using the ropes.

▷ Place floor mats beneath the ropes.

▷ Use an adult spotter for difficult stunts.

▷ Always have a teacher present.

▷ Check the ropes for frays or other worn-out areas.

Variations

▷ See descriptions of individual activities for possible variations.

▷ For a cross-curricular approach, use these activities in science when discussing the concepts of force and strength, or in health class when discussing muscles and bones or fitness.

Assessment

▷ Have children set goals for the number of letters they can form and repetitions they can perform.

▷ Discuss the importance of upper body strength in everyday situations.

JACK BE NIMBLE

Objectives

To improve bone and muscle strength; to help children learn the following movement concepts: transfer of weight, change of direction, relationships, and effort

Equipment Needed

▷ Floor mats

▷ Station signs to indicate the name of the activity at each station

Setup

Make sure you have enough space for children to perform activities and travel. If working with a whole group of children, scatter mats all about the gym floor. If working with small groups of children, create four station areas identified by station signs. Place mats at the station locations.

Instructions

Agility skills in developmental level 2 build on the strength and skills gained through doing developmental level 1 activities. Children at developmental level 2 tend to enjoy more partner activities. Teachers should place a greater emphasis on the quality of the movements performed. All four activities need to be done on floor mats.

Rolling Log. Starting in a push-up position on the mat or floor and keeping one hand and legs on the floor and their body straight, children swing their other arm up and over while turning the body. Once the first hand reaches the floor, they swing the other hand up and over their body, turning over again to regain the starting position.

Front Support to Stand. In a front support or push-up position on the mat or floor, children shift their body to a squatting position and then jump to a stand.

Forward Drop. Standing with their arms out in front of their body, children fall forward and, on contacting the floor mat with their hands, let their hands and arms bend to absorb the momentum. *Variations:* Repeat the forward drop but have one leg slightly raised while falling. An easier progression is to start from a kneeling position on the mat and drop onto hands before moving to a standing start.

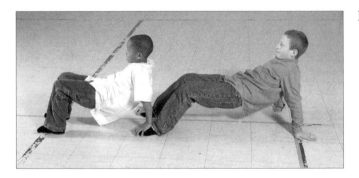

Partner Crab Walk. Child 1 is in a crab walk position. Child 2 assumes the same position directly in front of child 1, with hands resting on his or her feet and ankles. The two children try to move in a forward or backward direction without breaking contact.

Safety Considerations

▷ Allow children to rest between activities.

▷ Do not have children do any exercise if you are not comfortable with the level of safety present.

Variations

▷ See descriptions of individual activities for possible variations.

▷ For a cross-curricular approach, use these activities in science when discussing the concepts of absorption of force and strength.

Assessment

Observe children for proper form.

LIMBER UP!

Objectives

To improve bone and muscle strength; to help children become familiar with the following movement concepts: transfer of weight, change of direction, relationships, and effort

Equipment Needed

▷ Floor mats

▷ Station signs to indicate the name of the activity at each station

Setup

If working with a whole group of children, scatter mats all about the gym floor. If working with small groups of children, create four station areas identified by station signs. Place mats at the station locations. Children may work on the mats or floor with a partner.

Instructions

The Coffee Grinder. In a side-leaning position with one hand on the floor mat and the other hand extended upward and keeping the body straight, children walk slowly around and try to make a full circle turn. Repeat with other arm. *Variations:* Try going backward. Try to keep a beanbag balanced on the side of the body that faces upward.

Partner Pull-Up. Child 1 lies on the floor with knees bent and arms extended upward. Child 2 stands at the feet of child 1, grabs his or her hands, and rocks back, pulling him or her up until they have changed positions. *Variation:* Do this exercise on one foot.

Inchworm. In a squatting position, children take short steps with their hands until their legs and back are straight. Next, without moving the arms, they take short steps with their legs until they are back in the squatting position. *Variation:* Use one leg only.

Back to Back. Partners sit back to back with their arms and elbows locked, their knees bent, and their feet flat on the floor. On the count of three, partners push back against each other and attempt to stand up off of the floor. *Variation:* Stop halfway up and walk in different directions.

Safety Considerations

▷ Allow for children to rest between activities.

▷ Ensure cooperation between partners.

▷ If circumstances cause you to have a concern about the safety of any exercise, skip the exercise until you are comfortable using it.

Variations

▷ See descriptions of individual activities for possible variations.

▷ For a cross-curricular approach, use these activities in science when discussing the concepts of force and strength or when discussing Newton's law of action and reaction.

Assessment

▷ Watch for proper form.

▷ Observe for communication and cooperation among partners.

ROPE MAGIC

Objectives

To improve bone and muscle strength; to promote jumping and swinging skills; to help children become familiar with the movement concepts of weight transfer, change of direction, levels, and shapes

Equipment Needed

▷ Climbing ropes

▷ Floor mats

▷ Balance beam, piled mats, or bench

Setup

Place floor mats beneath climbing ropes. Place a bench or balance beam at the outer edge of the floor mats.

Instructions

Rope work involves climbing, swinging, and movement skills that children at all developmental stages can enjoy. Rope work is very beneficial to strengthening arm and shoulder muscles. It is important for children to progress at their own level when performing rope skills. These rope skills are an extension of the activities listed in the developmental level 1 gymnastics rope skills lesson. If children lack sufficient strength to perform these activities, have them perform the skills listed for developmental level 1.

Tuck Jump. In a standing position facing the rope, children jump up, grasp the rope, and bring their knees to their chest. *Variation:* Have legs go above the head.

Hand and Leg. In a standing position facing the rope, children jump up, grasp the rope, and wrap their legs around it. They hold the rope for a few seconds, then release. *Variations:* Release right hand, then left hand, or release right hand and right leg, and so on.

Skin the Cat. Start from a standing position. After reaching up and grasping the rope, children pull their legs up over their head so they are in a back hang position. Have them hold the position a few seconds and then return to the starting position.

Tarzan Swing. With a bench, balance beam, or piled mats in place, children bring the rope back to the bench, stand on the bench, and face forward. They then swing forward and drop off at the end of the upswing onto the floor mat. *Variations:* Swing back and land on the bench, or swing forward and tuck knees to the chest.

Safety Considerations

▷ Make sure children have warmed up and stretched their arm and shoulder muscles before using the ropes.

▷ For children at lower developmental levels, move the bench or balance beam closer to the climbing rope.

▷ Place floor mats beneath the ropes and next to benches or balance beams.

▷ Use an adult spotter for difficult stunts.

▷ The instructor should always be present.

▷ Check the ropes for frays or other worn areas.

Variations

▷ See descriptions of individual activities for possible variations.

▷ For a cross-curricular approach, use these activities in science when discussing the concepts of force and strength or when discussing flexibility and fitness in a health class or unit.

Assessment

Discuss the importance of developing upper body strength.

WEIGHT OF THE WORLD

Objectives

To improve bone and muscle strength; to help children become familiar with the concepts of balance and weight transfer

Equipment Needed

▷ Floor mats

▷ Station signs to indicate the name of the activity at each station

Setup

If working with a whole group of children, scatter mats all about the gym floor. If working with small groups, create four station areas identified by station signs. Place mats at the station locations.

Instructions

Children at this developmental level should see an increase in strength from developmental level 1. Balancing skills are beneficial for developing strength. All movements should be done slowly until the balance is accomplished. Have children hold each balance for three seconds. Do all four activities on floor mats.

Teddy Bear Stand. Ask children to form a triangle on the mat with their forehead and hands (make sure the triangle has the hands on the same side as the face, not behind the head). They then slowly walk their feet forward until their knees are near their elbows. At this point, they slowly raise their knees onto their elbows and hold the position.

Ankle Stand. One partner sits on a floor mat while the other stands straddled over the partner at about waist level. The standing partner bends and grasps onto the seated partner's ankles or puts both hands on the floor. The seated partner grasps onto the standing partner's legs and raises them above his or her head. The upper partner moves to a straight-leg and straight-back position. The finished position has the partner who is on top now in a push-up start position. Have children switch positions and repeat.

Frog Stand. With hands on the mat and fingers spread wide apart and pointed forward, children squat with arms straight and knees on the outside of their elbows. They slowly lean forward and press their elbows against their thighs and their thighs against their elbows. As their feet rise off the ground, they lower their head and trunk until they are in a balanced position. *Variations:* Lean forward, put chin on chest, and lower body to perform a forward roll. Lean forward, place the forehead on the mat, raise legs straight into the air and perform a headstand.

Push-Up Stand. One partner is in a hand–knee (all fours) balance position while the other is in front in a push-up position but with legs resting on the shoulders and back of his or her partner.

Safety Considerations

▷ Ensure that children are performing the movements slowly.

▷ Ensure cooperation between partners.

▷ Allow children to rest between activities.

▷ If you have a concern about the safety of any of the exercises, do not use that exercise. Use only those exercises you are comfortable with.

▷ For this set of exercises and any others in which children rest their weight on one another, make sure partners are of similar height and weight.

Variations

▷ See descriptions of individual activities for possible variations.

▷ For a cross-curricular approach, use these activities in science when discussing the concept of balance.

Assessment

▷ Observe children for proper form.

▷ Observe communication and cooperation among partners.

BALANCING

Developmental Level **3**

Objectives

To improve bone and muscle strength; to promote balance and the learning of movement concepts of weight transfer and relationships

Equipment Needed

> ▷ Floor mats
> ▷ Station signs to indicate the name of the activity at each station

Setup

If working with a whole group of children, scatter mats all about the gym floor. If working with small groups, create three station areas identified by station signs. Place mats at the station locations.

Instructions

The balance skills in developmental level 3 are an extension from the first two developmental levels. Balances at this level are excellent for strengthening the body.

V-Sit. Sitting on a floor mat with their knees bent and their feet flat on the ground, children grasp their ankles and slowly straighten their knees, extending their legs while balancing on their buttocks. *Variations:* Hold onto the toes. Extend arms sideways.

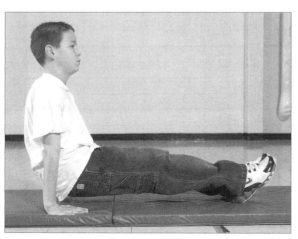

L-Support. Sitting on a floor mat with their legs together and pointed straight out in front, children place their hands on the ground below their shoulders and next to their body. They then press down and raise their hips and legs off the floor.

Flying Dutchman. Child 1 lies on a floor mat and extends arms up, with knees bent and feet in the air. Child 2 faces child 1, grasps his or her hands, and places his or her belly against child 1's feet. Child 1 extends legs to raise child 2 to a balanced position. Child 2 then straightens legs and body into a flying position. Once balance is achieved, hands can be momentarily released to simulate flying. Use a spotter when doing this exercise. *Variation:* Restrict the activity to holding hands at all times to better support the top partner.

Safety Considerations

▷ Ensure children are comfortable with the skills and progress at their own pace.

▷ Ensure cooperation between children to support each other during partner activities.

▷ If you have a concern about the safety of any of the exercises, do not use the exercise. Use only those exercises you are comfortable with.

Variations

▷ See descriptions of individual activities for possible variations.

▷ For a cross-curricular approach, use these activities in science when discussing the concept of balance.

Assessment

▷ Observe children for proper form.

▷ Ask children how they can make each balance more aesthetically pleasing.

COOPERATIVE MOVES

Objectives

To improve bone and muscle strength; to promote hopping skills; to help children understand the following movement concepts: weight transfer, change of direction, relationships, and effort

Equipment Needed

> Floor mats
> Station signs to indicate the name of the activity at each station

Setup

If working with a whole group of children, scatter mats all about the gym floor. If working with small groups, create four station areas identified by station signs. Place mats at the station locations. Each child works with a partner.

Instructions

These exercises are a continuation of the agility skills presented in developmental levels 1 and 2. The main focus of these activities is for children to work cooperatively on promoting bone and muscle development.

Wheelbarrow. For this activity, children should be placed with a partner who shares similar size and strength characteristics. One partner assumes the push-up position on the floor or mat while the other grasps the ankles of the first partner, lifting his or her legs off the ground. The first partner moves around using his or her arms while the other partner helps keep the first partner's legs in the air. *Variation:* The Double Wheelbarrow has the first child on hands and knees. The second child is in front of the first and rests his or her legs on the first child's back. A third child picks up the first child's ankles, and all three children attempt to move simultaneously.

Centipede. For this activity, children should be placed in groups of three and share similar size and strength characteristics. The first child gets down on hands and knees on the floor or mat. The second child moves in front of the first and places his or her hands on the floor or mat and then his or her legs onto the back and shoulders of the first child. A third child moves in front of the second child and repeats the same steps as the second child. The group then travels together (like a centipede) along the floor or mats, with the first child using feet and hands and the other two using their hands only. *Variation:* Walk backward, sideways, and turn around.

Heads Together! Partners are in a push-up position on the floor or mats with their heads touching. They attempt to rotate in a circle without losing contact. *Variations:* Change directions. Try doing push-ups without breaking contact. Raise one hand or leg off of the floor without breaking contact.

Partner Hopping. Partners stand facing each other and both raise their right leg so that the other partner can take hold of it with his or her left hand. Using the free arm for balance, the partners begin hopping gently to the left, then the right. *Variations:* One partner hops backward while the other hops forward. Change leg positions.

Safety Considerations

▷ Partners should be of similar height, weight, and strength for these activities.

▷ Ensure children are comfortable with the skills.

▷ Ensure partner holding feet in the wheelbarrow activity does not "push" the wheelbarrow but merely "supports" the wheelbarrow as it moves forward by itself.

▷ Ensure cooperation occurs to support each other during the activities.

▷ If you have a concern about the safety of any of the exercises, do not use the exercise. Use only those exercises you are comfortable with.

Variations

▷ See descriptions of individual activities for possible variations.

▷ For a cross-curricular approach, use these activities in social studies when discussing cooperation, communication, and supporting one another.

Assessment

▷ Observe children for proper form.

▷ Observe for cooperative behavior.

▷ Ask children what skills were easiest to perform and why.

REACH FOR THE TOP!

Objectives

To improve bone and muscle strength; to promote climbing skills; to help children understand the movement concepts of weight transfer, change of direction, and levels

Equipment Needed

- ▷ Climbing ropes
- ▷ Floor mats

Setup

Place floor mats beneath climbing ropes.

Instructions

These activities are an extension of the first two rope-climbing lessons for developmental levels 1 and 2. Children might need to perform the rope-climbing activities in the first two developmental levels before acquiring sufficient strength to perform these activities.

Photo courtesy Graham Fishburne

Photo courtesy Graham Fishburne

Stirrup Climb. Holding the rope with one hand above the other, children pull their body up, letting the rope rest on the left side of their body. They then pass the rope under their left foot and over their right foot. To move upward, they release the pressure off their feet and pull themselves up. To move down, they move hand under hand and control the pressure with the rope against their feet.

Scissors Climb. Standing with their left leg forward, children reach up and grab the rope at as high a point as they can reach. They then raise their back leg, bend at the knee, and place the rope inside their knee and outside their foot. They cross their forward leg over their back leg and then straighten both legs. To climb, they raise their knees up to their chest with the rope sliding between them. They lock the rope between their legs and climb using the hand-over-hand method. They then bring their knees to their chest and repeat the action. To lower themselves, they keep the pressure on their feet and move hand under hand until their knees are bent. They then lower their legs and repeat.

Photo courtesy Graham Fishburne

Photo courtesy Graham Fishburne

Foot and Leg Climb. Grasping the rope with one hand slightly above the other, children pull their body up and loop the rope over the top of their right foot. They place the left foot on top of the rope so that it is now locked into position. They then pull their body up and repeat the upward movement. To move down, they maintain the locked position and move hand under hand until their knees are at their chest. They hold their grip and lower their legs until they are extended, keeping the rope trapped between their feet. They then continue until reaching the floor.

Safety Considerations

▷ Make sure all children have warmed up and stretched their arm and shoulder muscles before using the ropes.

▷ Place mats beneath the ropes.

▷ A ribbon or marker can be tied to the climbing rope to indicate the maximum height allowed to be climbed.

▷ Use an adult spotter for difficult stunts.

▷ The instructor should always be present.

▷ Check the ropes for frays or other worn areas.

Variation

For a cross-curricular approach, use these activities in science when discussing the concepts of balance, strength, force, or gravity.

Assessment

▷ Observe children for proper form.

▷ Discuss the importance of upper body strength to overall fitness.

THE SKILL'S THE LIMIT!

Objectives

To improve bone and muscle strength; to promote jumping skills; to help children understand the movement concepts of transfer of weight, change of direction, relationships, and effort

Equipment Needed

▷ Floor mats

▷ Station signs to indicate the name of the activity at each station

Setup

If working with a whole group of children, scatter mats all about the gym floor. If working with small groups of children, create four station areas identified by station signs. Place mats at the station locations.

Instructions

The agility skills in developmental level 3 are an extension of the first two developmental levels. These skills are more complex movements, so be sure to give children adequate practice time to develop these skills.

Heel Click. From a semicrouched position with their arms at their sides, children jump up, click their heels together, and return to the starting position. *Variations:* Jump off one foot only, or run and then jump to click heels.

Seal Clap. From a push-up position on the floor or mat, children push off the floor with their hands and toes and clap their hands in the air before returning to the starting position. *Variation:* Try to clap twice.

Jump-Through. From a push-up or front support position, children shift their legs forward between their arms to a back support position. *Variation:* Walk through the movement.

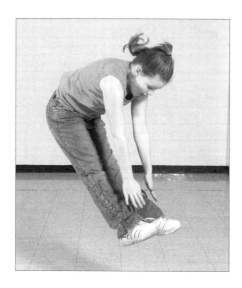

Jackknife. From a semicrouched position with their arms extended forward, children jump up and raise their legs, touching their toes with their hands before returning to the starting position. *Variation:* From the semicrouched start position, jump in the air and perform another shape before landing.

Safety Considerations

▷ Make sure children are comfortable with the exercises.

▷ Emphasize that the jumping action is to jump as *high* as possible. You do not want children to transfer their actions into a running long jump.

Variations

▷ See descriptions of individual activities for possible variations.

▷ For a cross-curricular approach, use these activities in science when discussing the concepts of balance, strength, force, or gravity.

Assessment

▷ Observe children for proper form.

▷ Ask children what skills were easiest to perform and why. Have them record their answers in an activity log or journal.

CHAPTER 4

DANCE ACTIVITIES

Dances use a variety of locomotor skills including jumping, hopping, galloping, and skipping that can help promote bone and muscle development in children. Dance also promotes strength, endurance, rhythm, balance, and creativity and presents many opportunities to integrate subjects within a curriculum. A wide variety of cultural backgrounds are reflected in dance, offering opportunities to recognize and appreciate diversity in our multicultural society. Finally, dance is also quite versatile, ranging from the personal expression of one or two individuals to extravagantly lavish group productions.

Because we usually suggest musical accompaniment for the dance activities that follow, dances have been broken down by measure. A measure is an equal grouping of underlying beats, or pulses, within the music. The time signature of the musical work tells how many beats make up a measure. In a 4/4 time signature, for example, four beats make up one complete measure. In a waltz with a 3/4 time signature, three beats make up one measure. Many of the dances presented in the chapter correspond to music counted in a 4/4 time signature.

Developmental Levels

- **Developmental Level 1.** Dances in this developmental level involve simple steps and movements and are usually done in a single-circle formation. These dances are the building blocks to more complex dances found in developmental levels 2 and 3.
- **Developmental Level 2.** Folk, line, and square dances are performed in various formations and involve more complex movement patterns and dance steps, increasing the length and effort necessary to perform them.
- **Developmental Level 3.** In this level, children are involved in more complex dance steps, such as the polka, schottische, and two-step, which typically require more skill and form than dances in the first two developmental levels do.

Rhythm

Rhythm is the ability to repeat an action or movement with regularity and in time to a particular pattern. For children to enjoy and experience success in dances, they need to have developed a sense of rhythm. Once children understand the elements of rhythm, they can learn other dance activities with greater speed and usually with a more positive attitude. We recommend involving young children in a program of rhythmic and movement activities before engaging them in the dances included in this chapter. Many good teaching resources are available that provide guidance in developmentally appropriate activities to help develop rhythmic awareness in young children (e.g., Kirchner & Fishburne, 1998).

Assessing Dance

To assess or evaluate dance activities, teachers should develop their own rubrics and checklists. The checklists provided in appendix B will assist you in assessing proficiency in many of the motor skills involved in the dances presented in this chapter. To supplement the checklists, appropriately designed rubrics are also helpful in assessing dance. A dance rubric should clearly define the performance criteria and differentiate among levels of performance. The rubric should also clearly define what children will be expected to do for maximum and minimum levels of achievement. An example of a rubric for assessing dance is provided in appendix B. Observation should identify those children who need extra help to develop a better sense of rhythm. To accommodate those who might need activities adjusted to their developmental level, match these children with partners most likely to aid them. Also, whenever possible, allow for individual creativity of movements so that lower levels of movement proficiency can be substituted into the dances to allow these children full participation.

CHILDREN'S POLKA

Objectives

To improve bone and muscle strength; to promote hopping, running, and sliding skills while learning to perform the German Kinderpolka (children's polka) folk dance

Equipment

▷ Musical reference: Children's Polka

▷ Lloyd Shaw Foundation. Internet access: www.lsda.org/index.html

Instructions

Group in partners, with girls on the right, and hold hands. All children form a double circle with boys on the inside, girls on the outer circle (all facing counterclockwise).

Part I

Measures 1–2	Start by having children take two slides toward center and step lightly three times.
Measures 3–4	Then take two slides away from center, returning to the starting position, and step lightly three times.

Part II

Measures 5–8	Repeat the actions of measures 1–4.
Measures 9–10	Once children are at the starting position again, they slap their own knees once, clap their own hands once, and then turn and clap their partner's hands three times.
Measures 11–12	Repeat the actions of measures 9–10.

Part III

Measure 13	Children hop and place their right heel forward, then place their right elbow in their left hand, and shake their finger three times.
Measure 14	Repeat the action of measure 13, but children now use their left foot.

Part IV

Measures 15–16	Finish by having children turn in place with four running steps and then stepping lightly three times with both feet.

Variations

▷ In part IV, replace stepping lightly three times with a heavier foot-stomping action. Replace four running steps with four vertical feet-together jumps.

▷ For a cross-curricular approach, use this folk dance activity in social studies when studying the customs and traditions of Germany. The counting of steps in this dance can benefit math practice in numeration and basic counting.

Assessment

Develop and use an assessment rubric for this folk dance. See appendix B for an example of a dance rubric.

DANISH DANCE OF GREETING

Objectives

To improve bone and muscle strength; to promote running and stomping skills; to help children learn and practice change of direction while learning the Danish Dance of Greeting

Equipment

▷ Musical reference: Danish Dance of Greeting

▷ Lloyd Shaw Foundation. Internet access: www.lsda.org/index.html

Instructions

In pairs of boys and girls, children stand in one large circle, facing the center with the girl on the right side of the boy.

Measure 1	Start by having children clap twice and turn and bow to their neighbors on either side.
Measure 2	Repeat but turn and bow to partner.
Measure 3	Stomp with the right foot, then stomp with the left foot.
Measure 4	Children then turn around, taking four running steps.
Measures 5–8	Repeat the actions of measures 1–4.
Measures 9–12	Finally, all join hands and run to the right for four measures (16 counts and 16 short running steps).
Measures 13–16	Repeat the actions of measures 9–12 but in the opposite direction to the left.

Variations

▷ In measure 4, replace the four running steps with hopping, skipping, or two-foot jumps.

▷ For a cross-curricular approach, use this folk dance activity in social studies when studying the customs and traditions of Denmark. The counting of steps in this dance can benefit math practice in numeration and basic counting.

Assessment

Develop and use an assessment rubric for this folk dance. See appendix B for an example of a dance rubric.

JUMP JIM JO

Objectives

To improve bone and muscle strength; to promote jumping, running, walking, and sliding skills; to help children gain familiarity in the movement concepts of change of direction and social relationships while learning the American circle dance Jump Jim Jo

Equipment

▷ Musical reference: Children's Folk Dances

▷ Artist: Georgiana Stewart

▷ Kimbo Educational. Internet access: www.kimboed.com

Instructions

In partners, the class forms two large circles, with partners joining hands to face each other. The following is a description of the steps involved.

Measures 1–2	Start with two jumps sideways, moving counterclockwise, followed by three quick jumps in place (slow, slow, fast, fast, fast).
Measures 3–4	Children release hands and turn one time around in place with four jumps. Partners should be facing each other when finished, rejoining hands.
Measure 5	Take two sliding steps counterclockwise.
Measure 6	Partners face counterclockwise with inside hands joined and tap three times with the toe of the outside foot.
Measures 7–8	Finish by taking four running steps forward, facing partner, joining hands, and ending with three jumps in place.

Variations

▷ Children can perform this dance individually, without a partner.

▷ For a mixer, have partners take four running steps to the right to meet a new partner, then jump three times in place.

▷ For a cross-curricular approach, use this circle dance activity in social studies when studying the customs and traditions of American people. The counting of steps in this dance can benefit math practice in numeration and basic counting.

Assessment

▷ Develop and use an assessment rubric for this folk dance. See appendix B for an example of a dance rubric.

▷ Observe for cooperative behavior.

▷ Discuss with children the movements that occurred and the health benefits of performing dances with jumping and stomping actions.

LET YOUR FEET GO TAP, TAP, TAP

Objectives

To improve bone and muscle strength; to promote stomping and skipping skills while learning the English singing dance Let Your Feet Go Tap, Tap, Tap

Equipment

> Musical reference: Let Your Feet Go Tap, Tap, Tap

> Lloyd Shaw Foundation. Internet access: www.lsda.org/index.html

Instructions

Have children form a double circle with partners facing each other, boys on the inside and girls on the outside.

Verse

Measures 1–2	Children stomp their feet on the ground three times on "tap, tap, tap."
Measures 3–4	Children clap their hands three times on "tap, tap, tap."
Measures 5–6	Children waggle fingers back and forth.
Measures 7–8	Children join hands and face counterclockwise.

Chorus

Measures 1–2	Children skip around the circle singing the chorus.
Measures 3–4	Children skip around the circle singing the chorus.
Measures 5–6	Children skip around the circle singing the chorus.
Measures 7–8	Children skip around the circle singing the chorus.

Variations

> Replace the skipping action in the chorus section with hopping and jumping in place.

> For a cross-curricular approach, use this singing dance activity in social studies when studying the customs and traditions of England. You can also use this dance and song in music class.

Assessment

Develop and use an assessment rubric for this singing dance activity. See appendix B for an example of a dance rubric.

WHOOMP DANCE

Objectives

To improve bone and muscle strength; to promote jumping and sliding skills; to aid children in learning the concept of change of direction while learning the Whoomp Dance

Equipment

▷ Musical reference: Whoomp (There It Is)

▷ 1993, Arista Records. Artist: Tag Team

Instructions

This popular song emphasizes jumping and sliding. Children might opt to perform a grapevine step instead of the slide. Start with the children in a line or free formation.

Measures 1–8	Slide right and clap on 4 (4 counts)
	Slide left and clap on 4 (4 counts). Grapevine steps can be used instead (step to the right, put left foot behind, step right again, then touch left foot beside the right foot).
Measures 9–16	Four pumps while stepping forward, starting with the right foot (each step is two counts, so complete eight counts total). A "pump" refers to moving elbows back and forth, similar to a marching action, with each count.
Measures 17–24	Jump a quarter turn to the right (2 counts).
	Jump a half turn to the left (2 counts).
	Jump three quarter turns to the right (should now be facing opposite direction) (4 counts).

Begin dance again, facing the opposite wall.

Variations

▷ For a cross-curricular approach, use this dance activity in math to practice counting.

▷ Have children create their own arm movements to replace the pumping action in measures 9 through16.

Assessment

Develop and use an assessment rubric for the Whoomp Dance. See appendix B for an example of a dance rubric.

BLEKING

Objectives

To improve bone and muscle strength; to promote hopping skills; to help children become familiar with the movement concepts of effort and relationships while learning the Swedish Bleking dance

Equipment

> ▷ Musical reference: Bleking
> ▷ Lloyd Shaw Foundation. Internet access: www.lsda.org/index.html

Instructions

Children begin in a circle formation with partners facing each other. Boys face counterclockwise, and girls face clockwise. Partners extend arms at shoulder height and join hands.

Measures 1–8	Children hop on left foot and extend the right heel forward, keeping the right leg straight. As this movement takes place, they thrust the right arm forward and pull the left arm back (count 1). Continue for seven more counts, changing the lead foot on each count.
Measures 9–16	Next, partners face each other and extend their arms sideways, joining hands. One partner (boy) begins with the right foot, and the other (girl) with the left foot. Partners begin to turn in place by taking seven step hops in a clockwise direction and end with a stamp on the last count. As the children turn in place, their arms move in a windmill action up and down with each step hop.

Repeat dance in counterclockwise direction.

Variations

> ▷ Replace the stamp in measures 9 through 16 with a two-foot jump.
> ▷ During the second part of the song, have children leave their partners and step-hop in various directions around the dancing area. When the music is about to change back to the first part of the song, have children find a new partner.
> ▷ For a cross-curricular approach, use this activity in social studies when studying the customs and traditions of Sweden.

Assessment

Develop and use an assessment rubric for this folk dance. See appendix B for an example of a dance rubric.

CSHEBOGAR

Objectives

To improve bone and muscle strength; to promote jumping, skipping, sliding, and walking skills while learning the Hungarian Cshebogar dance

Equipment

▷ Musical reference: Cshebogar

▷ Lloyd Shaw Foundation. Internet access: www.lsda.org/index.html

Instructions

Children begin by holding hands with a partner. All children then form a large circle and face the center.

Measures 1–4   Children take seven slide steps to the left and end with a jump on both feet.

Measures 5–8   Take seven slide steps to the right and end with a jump on both feet.

Measures 9–12   Take four walking steps to the center, raising hands high in the air. Take four walking steps back to original spot, lowering hands as they return.

Measures 13–16   The Hungarian Turn: Partners face each other and place their right hand on each other's waist. Raise the left arm, pull away from the partner, and skip around him or her.

Measures 17–20   Partners face each other, joining hands with arms held at shoulder height. Slide four steps slowly toward the center of the circle, bending toward the center during the slide. One partner begins with the left foot, and the other begins with the right foot.

Measures 21–24   The children then do four-step draw steps outward (step-close-step).

Measures 25–28   Next, they do two draw steps in and two draw steps out.

Measures 29–32   Finish by doing the Hungarian Turn as described in measures 13–16. Then repeat the entire dance.

Variations

▷ Instead of the Hungarian Turn, children can choose to do an elbow swing.

▷ For a cross-curricular approach, use this activity in social studies when studying the customs and traditions of Hungary.

Assessment

Develop and use an assessment rubric for this Hungarian folk dance. See appendix B for an example of a dance rubric.

POP GOES THE WEASEL

Objectives

To improve bone and muscle strength; to promote skipping skills; to help children learn the concept of change of direction while learning the American Pop Goes the Weasel folk dance

Equipment

▷ Musical reference: Pop Goes the Weasel
▷ Lloyd Shaw Foundation. Internet access: www.lsda.org/index.html

Instructions

Form partners, with girl on partner's right. Join with another set of partners to make a set of two couples (four children total). Label couples 1 and 2. Stay in sets of four (two couples) and form a large circle. With girl still on partner's right, couples turn to face each other so that couple 1 face clockwise and couple 2 face counter-clockwise.

Measures 1–4	Join hands in a circle of four and circle left with eight skipping steps.
Measures 5–6	Walk two steps forward, raise joined hands, then walk two steps backward, lowering hands.
Measures 7–8	Number 1 couples raise their joined hands to form an arch as number 2 couples pass under it. Number 2 couples continue forward to meet new partners.

Repeat the entire dance.

Variations

Replace the skipping action in measures 1–4 with hopping. With each repeat of measures 1–8, change hopping foot.

Assessment

Develop and use an assessment rubric for this folk dance. See appendix B for an example of a dance rubric.

TROIKA

Objectives

To improve bone and muscle strength; to promote running skills and learning the movement concepts of change of direction and speed while learning the Russian Troika dance

Equipment Needed

▷ Musical reference: Children's Folk Dances

▷ Artist: Georgiana Stewart

▷ Kimbo Educational. Internet access: www.kimboed.com

Instructions

The Troika is a Russian dance that means "three horses" and involves the movements of running and stomping. Start with children in groups of three facing counterclockwise in a circle formation.

Measures 1–4	When you call out "Run forward!" children quickly run 16 steps forward.
Measures 5–6	When you call out "Outside under!" the center and inside partners raise joined hands, forming an arch, and run in place while the outside dancer uses 8 running steps to move in front of the center dancer, under the arch, and back around the center dancer to the starting position. The center dancer unwinds by turning under the arch.
Measures 7–8	When you call out "Inside under!" the movements of measures 5–6 are repeated, but this time the inside dancer turns under the arch.
Measures 9–12	When you call out "Circle left!" the set of three join hands and take 12 running steps, ending with three stomps in place.
Measures 13–16	Repeat the 12 running steps to the right, ending in a re-formed line and with three stomps in place.

Variations

▷ During the last measure, the center dancer can move forward while the other dancers stomp three times in place.

▷ For a cross-curricular approach, use this activity in social studies when studying the customs and traditions of Russia.

Assessment

Develop and use an assessment rubric for this Russian folk dance. See appendix B for an example of a dance rubric.

COTTON-EYED JOE

Objectives

To improve bone and muscle strength; to promote jumping skills and the movement concepts of change of direction and relationships while learning the American folk dance Cotton-Eyed Joe

Equipment

▷ Musical reference: Cotton-Eyed Joe

▷ Lloyd Shaw Foundation. Internet access: www.lsda.org/index.html

Instructions

This dance can be done individually, in partners, or in groups of four.

Measures 1–2   Starting with the left foot, cross the left foot in front of the right foot, then kick the left foot forward. With the right leg, do small jumps at the same time as the cross kick.

Measures 3–4   Stomp feet three times.

Measures 5–6   Cross the right foot in front of the left foot, then kick the right foot forward. With the left leg, do small jumps at the same time as the cross kick.

Measures 7–8   Stomp feet three times.

Measures 9–16   Repeat measures 1–8.

Measures 17–32   Finally, perform right two-steps counterclockwise beginning with the left foot. (Step, close, step: repeat eight times.)

Variations

▷ During measures 17 through 32, individuals or partners may perform other locomotor movements such as skipping and galloping in various directions.

▷ For a cross-curricular approach, use this American folk dance activity in social studies when studying the customs and traditions of the United States.

Assessment

Develop and use an assessment rubric for this American folk dance. See appendix B for an example of a dance rubric.

SCHOTTISCHE

Objectives

To improve bone and muscle strength; to promote hopping and skipping skills; to help children learn the movement concepts of change of direction and relationships while learning the Schottische dance

Equipment Needed

▷ Musical reference: Children's Folk Dances

▷ Artist: Georgiana Stewart

▷ Kimbo Educational. Internet access: www.kimboed.com

Instructions

Form partners with girl on partner's right and join hands. Facing counterclockwise, children form a double circle with boys on the inside and girls on the outside.

Measures 1–2	Partners start with their outside feet (boy's left and girl's right) and run forward three steps then hop on the outside foot and extend the inside foot forward.
Measures 3–4	Repeat the action but start with the inside foot.
Measures 5–6	Finish with both partners taking four step hops in place. Repeat the first six measures as often as desired.

Variations

▷ For measures 5 and 6, try these three variations:

• Ladies Turn: Boys take four step hops in place, and girls turn under their arms. On the next turn, reverse the movements, with boys turning under the girl's raised arms.

• Both Turn: Partners drop hands and dance four skip hops in place, turning away from each other (boy turns to the left, girl to the right) on the first step, and ending in the starting position on the fourth step hop.

• Wring the Dishrag: Partners join hands about waist high and both turn under raised arms and continue around and back to the starting position.

▷ For a cross-curricular approach, use this activity in social studies when studying the customs and traditions of Scotland.

Assessment

Develop and use an assessment rubric for this folk dance. See appendix B for an example of a dance rubric.

SEVEN JUMPS

Developmental Level **3**

Objectives

To improve bone and muscle strength; to promote jumping and hopping skills and learning of the movement concepts of change of direction and relationships while learning the Danish Seven Jumps dance

Equipment Needed

> ▷ Musical reference: Seven Jumps
> ▷ Lloyd Shaw Foundation. Internet access: www.lsda.org/index.html

Instructions

Start with all children joining hands to form a single circle.

Measures 1–8	Beginning with the left foot, take seven step hops, then jump and land with feet together on the eighth beat.
Measures 9–16	Face clockwise, start with the right foot and take seven step hops, then jump and land on both feet, facing the center.
Measures 17–18	All drop hands, place hands on hips, lift the right knee upward, stamp foot on floor, and join hands.
Measures 1–18	Repeat measures 1–18 but do not join hands.
Measure 19	Raise left knee, stamp foot, and join hands.
Measures 1–19	Repeat measures 1–19 but do not join hands.
Measure 20	Kneel on right knee, stand, and join hands.
Measures 1–20	Repeat measures 1–20 but do not join hands.
Measure 21	Kneel on left knee, stand, and join hands.
Measures 1–21	Repeat measures 1–21 but do not join hands.
Measure 22	Place right elbow on floor and cheek on right fist, then stand and join hands.
Measures 1–22	Repeat measures 1–22 but do not join hands.
Measure 23	Place left elbow on floor and cheek on left fist, then stand and join hands.
Measures 1–23	Repeat measures 1–23 but do not join hands.
Measure 24	Place forehead on floor, stand, and join hands.
Measures 1–16	Finish by repeating measures 1–16.

Variations

> ▷ This dance can be performed using a parachute. The dancers hold the parachute taut with one hand during the step hops and with both hands for all jumps except the last, during which the forehead touches the parachute on the floor.
> ▷ For a cross-curricular approach, use this activity in social studies when studying the customs and traditions of Denmark.

Assessment

Develop and use an assessment rubric for this Danish folk dance. See appendix B for an example of a dance rubric.

TINIKLING

Objectives

To improve bone and muscle strength; to promote jumping and stepping skills and the movement concepts of change of direction, speed, and relationships while learning the Philippine Tinikling folk dance

Equipment Needed

▷ Bamboo poles (or other poles, such as broom handles)

▷ Wooden blocks or boards of wood

▷ Any music with a 3/4 waltz meter

Instructions

In Tinikling dance, the dancer moves around two people who sit on the floor and manipulate two bamboo poles. The poles are placed 2 feet (.6 meters) apart and rest at right angles on the top of two boards or blocks of wood. The children holding the poles slide them across the boards and strike them together on the count of 1. On counts 2 and 3, they lift the poles about an inch (2.5 centimeters) off the boards, open them about 12 inches (30 centimeters) apart, and tap them twice against the boards. The music is a 3/4 waltz meter with a distinct "strike, tap, tap" rhythm throughout the dance.

The following Basic Step can be performed individually or in pairs. Once they have learned the Basic Step, children can develop their own combinations and routines (see Variations).

Basic Step

The dancer begins outside of the poles with his or her right side closest to the pole. With the 3/4 rhythm, the first step is performed outside of the poles as they are hit together. The next two steps are performed inside of the poles as they are tapped twice on the blocks. The pattern goes this way: step left (outside poles), step right (inside poles), step left (inside poles), step right (outside to the right side), and continue back.

Safety Considerations

Children handling the poles should focus on each other and not the dancer's feet to avoid any issues of raising the poles too high or too soon.

Variations

▷ Children may start with poles (or other objects such as jump ropes) remaining stationary.

▷ For a cross-curricular approach, use this folk dance activity in social studies when studying the customs and traditions of the Philippines.

▷ You might want to try the following two-step variations:

Straddle Step

The dancer performs two jumps with feet together inside the poles and a straddle jump when the poles are brought back together.

Forward and Backward Step

The dancer faces the poles, steps forward with the right foot inside the poles, then steps forward with the left foot. As the poles are brought together, the dancer takes a step forward on the right foot to the opposite side of the poles. The pattern is reversed on the next measure, with a step back on the left foot, followed by a step back with the right foot, and a step back with the left foot to the starting position.

Assessment

Develop and use an assessment rubric for this folk dance. See appendix B for an example of a dance rubric.

TUSH PUSH

Objectives

To improve bone and muscle strength; to promote jumping and stepping skills and learning the concept of change of direction while learning the Tush Push dance

Equipment Needed

Musical reference: "Trouble" by Travis Tritt

Instructions

Measure 1	Start by tapping the right heel forward, then move the right heel toward the left knee and tap the right heel forward twice.
Measure 2	Switch. Tap the left heel forward, then move the left heel toward the right knee and tap the left heel forward twice.
Measure 3	Jump right forward, left forward, right forward, and clap.
Measure 4	Bounce the right hip forward twice and left hip backward twice.
Measure 5	Swing hips clockwise twice.
Measure 6	Polka step forward: right, left, right, rock step (step forward on left foot, shift weight to right foot).
Measure 7	Polka backward: left, right, left, rock step (step backward on right foot, shift weight to left foot).
Measure 8	Polka forward: right, left, right, step forward on the left foot, pivot a half turn clockwise.
Measure 9	Again, polka forward: left, right, left, step forward on right foot, pivot a quarter turn counterclockwise.
Measure 10	Finish by pivoting a quarter turn counterclockwise, pivot again another quarter turn counterclockwise, stomp the right foot, and clap.

Repeat measures 1–10.

Variations

▷ Perform this dance to "Cadillac Ranch" by the Nitty Gritty Dirt Band.

▷ For a cross-curricular approach, use this folk dance activity in social studies when studying the customs and traditions of the United States.

Assessment

Develop and use an assessment rubric for this dance activity. See appendix B for an example of a dance rubric.

CHAPTER 5

SUPPLEMENTAL ACTIVITIES

In this chapter we provide additional activities that help children develop strong bones and muscles. You can integrate these activities into existing lessons or units of study or use them as fitness breaks for any time of the day. We also include a small selection of activities for the classroom setting. Note that many of the activities described in previous chapters can be easily adapted and used in the classroom or other indoor setting. In our view, instructors and teachers should use the classroom or other indoor setting whenever possible for physical activity—doing so shows children how easy it can be to engage in regular physical activity.

BOUNCE AT THE BELL

Objectives

To build strong bones and muscles

Equipment Needed

None

Instructions

What is Bounce at the Bell?

Bounce at the Bell is a physical activity program in which children do a series of daily jumps to enhance their bone strength.

Why should my class participate in Bounce at the Bell?

The Bounce at the Bell program is designed to help children build strong bones during their formative years and thus reduce the risk of osteoporosis bone fractures later in life. Children who participated in a Bounce at the Bell program over an eight-month period demonstrated enhanced bone health compared with children who did not participate. In British Columbia, Canada, 8- to 10-year-old children who participated in a Bounce at the Bell program over an eight-month period significantly increased bone mass compared to children of similar ages who attended schools that did not participate in the program. Bounce at the Bell is now an integral part of the Action Schools! BC initiative (www.actionschools.bc.ca), which is ongoing and has shown the positive benefits of physical activity for bone health and academic performance (McKay, Tsang, Heinonen, MacKelvie, Sanderson, & Khan, 2005).

When should my class bounce?

You can jump in the morning, during recess, or over lunch—there is no one best time. Many instructors opt to make a class jumping schedule to match their teaching schedule.

How many times should children bounce per session?

Children begin with 5 jumps, 3 times a day, 4 days a week. Each month they add another jump to each jumping session, so in their eighth month they reach 36 jumps per day.

What types of jumps should my class be doing?

Jumping Jack Flash, Leaping Lizards, Terrific Triathletes, and Disco Dancers, all described in chapter 1, are the four best jumps for most children to perform during Bounce at the Bell. Activity cards for these jumps can be found on pages 128 and 129. As a class, you can decide which of the four jumps to perform. Children need not vary their jumps if they choose not to. If they enjoy Leaping Lizards the most, they can perform this jump every time.

If your students are doing single-leg landings (Disco Dancer and Terrific Triathlete), then the number of jumps needs to be doubled to achieve the correct total of landings per leg. The chart on the next page indicates the progression of jumping for an

Month	Number of two-foot landing jumps at each bell (Jumping Jack Flash or Leaping Lizards)	Number of one-foot landing jumps at each bell (Terrific Triathletes or Disco Dancers)	Number of jumping sessions per day	Total number of jumps per day
October	5	10 (5 per leg)	3	15
November	6	12 (6 per leg)	3	18
December	7	14 (7 per leg)	3	21
January	8	16 (8 per leg)	3	24
February	9	18 (9 per leg)	3	27
March	10	20 (10 per leg)	3	30
April	11	22 (11 per leg)	3	33
May	12	24 (12 per leg)	3	36

eight-month time frame. (Note this example begins in October, but start and finish times can be adjusted to fit personal schedules.)

Remember that children should jump 5 times, 3 times a day, 4 times a week and add 1 jump each month, according to the chart.

Safety Considerations

▷ Ensure each child has enough space to perform the jumps safely.

▷ Remove all sharp and hard objects and equipment from the jumping and bouncing area.

▷ Do not allow children to jump or bounce close to desks or other furniture.

Variations

▷ The example shown in the chart is for children at developmental levels 2 and 3. Bounce at the Bell can also be used with developmental level 1 children, but the number of bounces (jumps) required should be reduced for these children. In general, younger children tire more quickly than older children, but they also recover more quickly, so they should do fewer jumps with less rest time between them.

▷ To accommodate differences in fitness levels, developmental levels, and general individual differences, use personal task cards to determine the most appropriate number of bounces.

▷ Use journals or personal activity log books for goal setting and to record student performances.

▷ For a cross-curricular approach, use Bounce at the Bell in science when discussing force, Newton's laws of action and reaction, and how the body works. You can also discuss in health class or a health unit in another class the benefits of performing Bounce at the Bell.

Assessment

▷ Watch for proper form in jumping.

▷ Ask students to name the health benefits associated with Bounce at the Bell.

▷ Record performances in journals and personal activity log books and compare to goals set on task cards.

LEAPING LIZARDS

Equipment

None

Starting Position

- Stand with legs together and hands at sides.

Action

- Jump into a tuck position.
- Land in a scissors step with legs bent.

From *Building Strong Bones & Muscles*, Graham Fishburne, Heather McKay, and Stephen Berg (2005). Champaign, IL: Human Kinetics.

DISCO DANCERS

Equipment

None

Starting Position

- Stand with one leg up and bent.

Action

- Jump from the leg on the floor to the other leg.
- Repeat with the other leg.
- Try to get as much height as possible on each jump.

From *Building Strong Bones & Muscles*, Graham Fishburne, Heather McKay, and Stephen Berg (2005). Champaign, IL: Human Kinetics.

TERRIFIC TRIATHLETES

Equipment

None

Starting Position

- Stand with feet shoulder-width apart.

Action

- Jump from side to side with full power.
- Swing arms, skating style.

From *Building Strong Bones & Muscles*, Graham Fishburne, Heather McKay, and Stephen Berg (2005). Champaign, IL: Human Kinetics.

JUMPING JACK FLASH

Equipment

None

Starting Position

- Stand with feet together.

Action

- Jump up high.
- Spread legs wide to land.
- Bring hands over head and clap.

From *Building Strong Bones & Muscles*, Graham Fishburne, Heather McKay, and Stephen Berg (2005). Champaign, IL: Human Kinetics.

Objectives

To improve bone and muscle strength using resistance bands

Equipment Needed

Elastic resistance bands

Instructions

These exercises can be done by themselves or in combination with others, or they can be incorporated into the resistance training circuit for developmental level 3 (see chapter 1). The exercises can be done in the classroom or any other area with enough space for children to use resistance bands.

Shoulder Front Raise

Starting Position

▷ From a seated position, grasp one end of an exercise band in one hand with palm facing inward, thumb to the ceiling, and elbow bent at 90 degrees.

▷ The other end of the band is placed under the foot on the same side so that the band is taut.

Action

▷ Lift and straighten the arm up in front of the body to shoulder level (no bend at the elbow).

▷ Hold this position for a count of two and then slowly return to the starting position.

▷ Children should do 5 to 10 repetitions with each arm.

Note: This exercise can be performed in a standing position with feet shoulder-width apart, knees slightly bent, and stomach muscles contracted.

Shoulder Single-Arm Lateral Raise

Starting Position

▷ From a seated position, grasp one end of the exercise band with each hand, shoulder-width apart at waist height, palms facing down.

Action

▷ Lift one arm out to the side of the body at shoulder level while keeping the elbow straight.

▷ Hold this position for a count of two and then slowly return to the starting position.

▷ Perform 5 to 10 repetitions.

▷ Repeat with the other arm.

Overhead Shoulder Press

Starting Position

▷ Sitting upright in a chair, place the exercise band under the buttocks and grasp one end of the band in each hand, thumbs facing upward.

▷ To start, elbows should be at 90 degrees to the side of the body with the band taut.

Action

▷ Raise hands above the head, maintaining a slight bend in the elbows at the end of the lift.

▷ Hold this position for a count of two and then slowly return to the starting position.

▷ Children should perform 5 to 10 repetitions.

Chest Pull

Starting Position

▷ In a seated or standing position, grasp the exercise band with hands shoulder-width apart and palms facing downward.

▷ Lift the arms out in front of the body at shoulder height with a slight bend in the elbows.

Action

▷ Squeeze the shoulder blades together while pulling the band laterally to the sides, maintaining shoulder height.

▷ Hold this position for a count of two and then slowly return to the starting position.

▷ Children should perform 5 to 10 repetitions.

Incline Press

Starting Position

▷ In a seated or standing position, grasp the exercise band with one hand and place it on the opposite hip.

▷ Hold the other end of the band with the arm at shoulder level.

Action

▷ Press the top hand upward above the head until the arm is fully extended.

▷ Hold this position for a count of two and then slowly return to the starting position.

▷ Repeat with the other arm.

▷ Children should do 5 to 10 repetitions with each arm.

Lat Pull-Down

Starting Position

▷ In a seated or standing position, grasp the exercise band with both hands shoulder-width apart.

▷ Raise arms straight overhead.

▷ Ensure the band is taut.

Action

▷ While keeping tension on the band, pull the arms down behind the head to shoulder level.

▷ Hold this position for a count of two and then slowly return to the starting position.

▷ Children should do 5 to 10 repetitions.

Leg Extension

Starting Position

▷ In a seated position with knees at 90 degrees, make a loop at one end of the exercise band and place it around one foot.

▷ Wrap the band two times around the bottom leg of a chair and hold onto the other end of the exercise band with the opposite hand.

Action

▷ Straighten the leg outward.

▷ Hold this position for a count of two and then slowly return to the starting position.

▷ Repeat with the other leg.

▷ Children should do 5 to 10 repetitions with each leg.

Plantar Flexion

Starting Position

▷ In a seated position, grasp one end of the exercise band in each hand and place the middle of the band around the balls of the feet.

▷ Legs are extended out straight and toes are pointed toward the ceiling.

Action

▷ Press feet toward the floor. (Make sure the band doesn't slip off the foot!)

▷ Hold this position for a count of two and then slowly return to the starting position.

▷ Children do 5 to 10 repetitions.

Safety Considerations

▷ Ensure that all children have been shown the correct way to use resistance bands.

▷ Make sure the resistance bands are strong and free of rips and tears.

Variations

▷ Ask children to create new exercises using the resistance bands.

▷ Use journals or personal activity log books to set goals.

▷ Create personal task cards to individualize activities to the developmental level of the child.

▷ For a cross-curricular approach, use this activity in science to discuss force, elasticity, and strength.

Assessment

▷ Record student performances in a journal or personal activity log book.

▷ Check performances against personal "goals" set for the elastic resistance bands.

PARACHUTE ACTIVITIES

Objectives

To improve bone and muscle strength while participating in cooperative parachute activities

Equipment Needed

Parachute

© Human Kinetics

Instructions

Parachute activities provide an exciting component to any physical activity program. They provide fun and cooperation among participants and can incorporate weight-bearing activities for bone and muscular development. Parachutes are available in many sizes. Participants hold onto the handgrips provided around the periphery of the chute.

Wave Upon Wave. Children slowly begin to shake the parachute up and down. On a signal, they gradually shake the parachute faster and faster. When they are going their fastest, signal the children to begin slowing down until they are making gentle waves again. This activity can also be done kneeling.

Whoa, Horsey! Children face away from the parachute with one leg forward and hold onto the handgrips using an overhand grip. On the count of 3, children pull the chute as hard as they can for 10 seconds. Make sure feet are stationary. Try this in the kneeling position.

Pull-Outs. Using an underhand grip, children have one leg in front of the other facing the parachute. Feet remain stationary. On the count of three, all children pull the chute toward themselves as hard as they can and hold for 10 seconds. Repeat using the overhand grip or kneeling down.

Curl-Ups. All children are under the parachute in a curl-up position holding on with an overhand grip. The parachute is firmly held up to the chin. Holding this grip, children sit up to an upright position, then return to the starting position.

Popcorn. Place 5 to 8 small foam or sponge balls on the parachute. Children begin to shake the parachute, trying to keep the balls in the air for as long as they can.

V-Sit. Children lie on their backs with the top of their heads facing the parachute and palms facing forward, holding the chute. Keep the parachute tight, then raise the chest and straighten legs to a V-sit position. Return to the start.

Push-Ups. Children raise the parachute to form a mushroom, keeping their hands and knees on the edge of the parachute. They then extend their legs backward and perform a push-up. If this is too difficult, children can remain on their knees and perform a modified push-up.

Safety Considerations

Make sure any equipment used with the parachute, such as small balls, are made of sponge or foam.

Variations

▷ Invite children to invent their own parachute game.

▷ For a cross-curricular approach, use the parachute activities in science when discussing flotation, force, leverage, and strength.

Assessment

▷ Observe for cooperative behavior during activities.

▷ Observe for full participation by all children.

LONG ROPE-JUMPING CHALLENGES

Developmental Level (1)(2)(3)

Objectives

To improve bone strength and muscle strength through participation in rope-jumping activities

Equipment Needed

Long ropes for skipping or jumping rope

Instructions

Jumping is a high-impact, weight-bearing activity that can help develop strong bones and muscles. Different rope-jumping activities offer variety in jumping.

Jump the Rope. Two turners hold a long rope motionless so that the middle is 6 inches (15 centimeters) off the ground. Jumpers take turns going over the rope. Try for at least 10 jumps in a row, or children can turn or make shapes in the air as they go over the rope.

Rising Tide. Keeping the rope motionless, one turner holds the rope on the ground while the other turner holds the rope at waist height. Starting at the low end, the jumper moves up the rope, jumping higher and higher until reaching the high end of the rope.

Tick-Tock. The turners swing the rope back and forth, making a half turn only. The jumper can begin in the middle or run in from the side.

Long Rope Jumping. Turners swing the rope making full turn rotations. Jumper can begin in the middle, or start from the outside and run into the middle, and begin jumping over the rope.

Safety Considerations

Provide enough space between children to ensure no one is hit by a turning rope.

Variations

The following is a list of activities children can do to promote regular long rope jumping:

> Jump using one foot only for a count of five, then switch feet.
> Make a quarter, half, three-quarter, and then a full turn with each jump.
> Jump while slowly lowering the body into a squatting position, then return to regular jumping position.
> Have turners increase the speed of the rope to play "hot pepper."
> Jump with a ball and attempt to bounce the ball while jumping.
> Repeat the above skills with a partner.

▷ Play follow-the-leader with three or more children. First player jumps in, performs a stunt, and jumps out. The rest of the group repeats the first player's stunt.

▷ For a cross-curricular approach, use rope-jumping activities when discussing cardiovascular fitness and heart rate in health class or a health unit.

Assessment

▷ Observe for full participation by all children.

▷ Observe for cooperation among participants.

SHORT ROPE-JUMPING CHALLENGES

Developmental Level **1 2 3**

Objectives

To improve bone strength and muscular strength through short rope-jumping activities

Equipment Needed

A variety of sizes of jump ropes

Instructions

Letters and Numbers. This activity is good for developmental level 1. Students form letters and numbers on the floor with their ropes. Once they form a number or letter, have them jump in, out, and around the shape. Repeat for several letters or numbers.

Skier. Using a double-foot jump, stand with feet together and jump from side to side over a line on the floor as you jump over the rope.

Jogger. While the rope is turning, use a jogging-in-place technique, alternating feet.

Boxer. While the rope is turning, jump twice on the left foot, then twice on the right foot. Continue this pattern.

Backward. Turn the rope backward instead of forward.

Rocker. The rocker step always has one foot as the lead leg. As the rope passes under the lead foot, transfer the weight forward, raising the back foot so the rope passes under it. Rock back, transferring the weight to the lead foot.

One-Foot Hop. Perform a one-foot hop with each turn of the rope. Continue for a set number of hops on one leg, then switch legs.

Mountain Climber. Begin in a stride position with one leg in front of the other. As the rope passes underneath, jump in the air and reverse the position of the feet.

Heel-Toe Combo. On the first turn, the jumper touches the left heel to the floor. On the second turn, he or she touches the left toe next to the right foot. Repeat the same pattern with the right foot.

Skipping Jacks. With feet together and on the first turn of the rope, jump and move the legs shoulder-width apart. On the second turn, jump and move the legs back together.

Criss-Cross. Keeping the feet together as the rope is overhead, cross the arms, creating a loop. Jump through the loop and uncross the arms. As the rope turns overhead again, create another loop and repeat the pattern.

Pepper. Here, the rope passes under the jumper twice before he or she returns to the ground. The jumper will have to jump a little higher off the ground and turn the wrists quicker.

Safety Considerations

▷ Allow enough space between children to ensure swinging and turning ropes do not come into contact with participants.

▷ Ensure children have skipping ropes of a length appropriate to their height. They should be able to stand on the rope while placing the hand grips under their arms.

Variations

▷ Encourage children to create their own skipping routines.

▷ Use partners to copy or follow each other's skipping routine.

▷ For a cross-curricular approach, do rope jumping when discussing force, strength, and leverage in science or cardiovascular fitness and heart rate in health class.

Assessment

Observe for full participation by all children.

HOOP IT UP!

Developmental Level **1 2 3**

Objectives

To improve bone strength and muscle strength through participation in hoop games

Equipment Needed

▷ Hoops
▷ Music and music source

Instructions

Hoop games provide opportunities to incorporate jumping into game activities. Jumping activities provide high-impact, weight-bearing opportunities that promote the development of strong bones and muscles.

1. Scatter hoops around the gym.
2. When you start the music, children begin to run slowly around the area, avoiding all hoops.
3. When the music stops, children must find a hoop and jump in it until the music starts again.
4. Play for a few minutes, then switch from running slowly to skipping, leaping, galloping, hopping, and so on.

Safety Considerations

▷ Allow enough space for children to move freely between hoops.
▷ Stress not landing on the hoop.
▷ Stress not stepping on the hoops when traveling between and around hoops.

Variations

▷ Children hop into and out of hoops.
▷ For a cross-curricular approach, use these hoop activities when discussing in science how the body works.

Assessment

▷ Observe for cooperative behavior.
▷ Observe for full participation by all children.

TAG GAMES

Objectives

To improve bone strength and muscle strength through participation in tag games

Equipment Needed

▷ Cones
▷ Pinnies

Instructions

Tag games provide opportunities to incorporate jumping into game activities. Jumping activities provide high-impact, weight-bearing opportunities for the development of strong bones and muscles.

Jump and Crouch Tag

1. Divide the class into four equal groups with pinnies or according to their shirt color.
2. All students scatter within the playing area. Boundaries can be floor lines or marked with cones.
3. Choose one of the four groups to be "it." The "it" group chases other players who, if caught, must wait for another player to touch them. Once they are touched, the player must perform five tuck jumps or other weight-bearing activity before returning to the game.
4. Play for a few minutes, then switch tagging group.
5. Stress proper jumping technique before starting the game.

Partner Tag

1. Group students in pairs.
2. Each student takes a turn being "it." On signal, each pair plays tag, with one student being "it" and trying to tag his or her partner.
3. If tagged, the partner must do five tuck jumps. He or she is now "it," and roles are reversed.
4. Play for a few minutes, then switch partners. Note, if one partner is much faster than the other restrict both partners to fast walking only.

Safety Considerations

▷ Stress the importance of safety when playing tag games: no slapping, shoving, or tripping.
▷ Remind children to watch out for each other when playing tag.
▷ Consider restricting children to walking in the first few tag games so they can learn to watch out for others and avoid accidents.

Variations

> ▷ Change the rules to accommodate children at different developmental levels. For example, limit younger children to walking.

> ▷ Allow children to come up with ideas to free each other once they have been tagged.

> ▷ For a cross-curricular approach, use these activities as examples of exercises to participate in to improve cardiovascular health and fitness during health classes.

Assessment

Observe for full participation by all children.

HEALTHY BONES HOTEL

Objective

To supplement knowledge of healthy bones and muscles through a cross-curricular and teamwork approach

Equipment Needed

▷ Paper

▷ Markers

▷ Pencil crayons

▷ Nutritional food guide

▷ Fitness resources

Setup

▷ Arrange students in groups of three or four.

▷ The students are managers of a healthy bones hotel. Their task as a group is to design a menu, exercise program, and promotional brochure for people who stay five days at the hotel.

Instructions

▷ The menu should include three meals a day and two snacks.

▷ The exercise program should be balanced and allow for muscle recovery.

▷ There should be a list of facilities and equipment you need at the hotel to aid in muscle and bone development.

▷ The promotional brochure should include key information about the hotel and a schedule of events; it should be colorful and neatly done.

Variation

For a cross-curricular approach, use this activity as part of a health unit to discuss nutrition awareness or as an art unit on graphic design.

Assessment

Make a school display of the Healthy Bones Hotel brochures.

JUMPING VOCABULARY

Objective

To supplement knowledge of healthy bones and strong muscles through a cross-curricular approach

Equipment Needed

▷ Thesaurus

▷ Dictionary

▷ Diagram of the muscular and skeletal system

Setup

Classroom or gym setting

Instructions

Have students use a thesaurus or dictionary to give new names to common exercises (for example, "curl-up" might become "warp rise"). Here are some exercises for them to try to rename:

Jumping jacks

Stride jumps

Step-ups

Curl-ups

Tuck jumps

Split jumps

Push-ups

Extension

Now have students create activity cards for their newly named exercises. You might help children get started with this list of action words:

Jump—bounce, spring

Hop—spring

Leap—spring, lunge, soar, hurdle

Gallop—stamp, prance

Run—dash, dart

Slide—slither, slip

Crawl—creep, swim, streak

Curl—bend, round, circle

Balance—anchor, solid, stable, hold

Upward—ascend, rise, climb

Downward—descend, slump, drop, sink

Variation

For a cross-curricular approach, use this activity for vocabulary development in language arts.

Assessment

Evaluate based on creativity and vocabulary of words chosen.

APPENDIX A

CROSS-CURRICULAR WORKSHEETS AND REPRODUCIBLES

Knowledge about bones and muscles can be easily gained through cross-curricular activities. In this appendix we provide a number of different curricular subject area activities designed to promote learning about bones and muscles.

Bone Busters!

Name_____ Date_____

Help the Bone Builders get away from the Bone Busters.

1. Look at each word in the middle column.

2. Is it something that is good for your bones? Is it something that might protect your bones? If it is, it is a Bone Builder. Write the word under Bone Builders.

3. If the word is something that is not good for your bones, write the word under Bone Busters.

Bone Builders	What am I?	Bone Busters
	Sunshine	
	Soda	
	Alcohol	
	Weight-bearing exercise	
	Dark, leafy vegetables	
	Fractures	
	Smoking	
	Yogurt	
	Falling	
	Being a couch potato	
	Calcium	
	Weightlessness	
	Caffeine	
	Jumping rope	
	Slippery places	
	Vitamin D	
	Milk	
	Cheese	

From *Building Strong Bones & Muscles,* Graham Fishburne, Heather McKay, and Stephen Berg (2005). Champaign, IL: Human Kinetics.

Name_____ Date_____

Circle the body parts that you use when you:

1. Jump

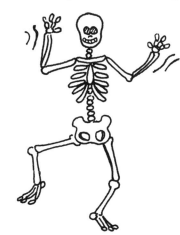

2. Gallop

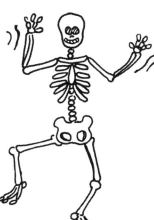

3. Jump rope

4. Seal crawl

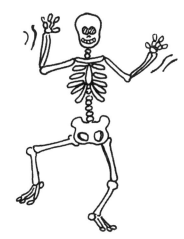

5. Do push-ups

6. Do curl-ups

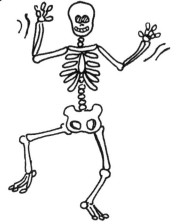

From *Building Strong Bones & Muscles,* Graham Fishburne, Heather McKay, and Stephen Berg (2005). Champaign, IL: Human Kinetics.

Name_____ Date_____

Each math question equals a letter. Use the letters to complete the answer to the following question:

How do you build healthy bones?

8 x 3= _____   7 x 4 =_____   6 x 5=_____   8 x 4=_____
      I   M   N   S

11 x 2=_____   2 x 4=_____   12 x 3=_____   9 x 1=_____
     R   U   E   A

13 x 5=_____   2 x 5=_____   10 x 10=_____   9 x 2=_____
     C   X   D   L

24 x 2=_____   6 x 7=_____   5 x 5=_____   4 x 10=_____
     G   B   T   O

__ __ __ __ __ __ __   __ __ __
65 9 18 65 24 8 28   9 30 100

__ __ __ __ __ __ __ __
36 10 36 22 65 24 32 36

__ __ __ __ __
42 8 24 18 100

__ __ __ __ __ __   __ __ __ __ __.
32 25 22 40 30 48   42 40 30 36 32

From Building Strong Bones & Muscles, Graham Fishburne, Heather McKay, and Stephen Berg (2005). Champaign, IL: Human Kinetics.

Name_____ Date_____

The answer to each math question equals a letter. At the bottom of the page, use the answers and corresponding letters to complete the answer to the following question:

How can you build strong bones and muscles?

$10 \div 2 =$ _____ W

$24 \div 8 =$ _____ I

$36 \div 9 =$ _____ G

$12 \div 6 =$ _____ E

$28 \div 2 =$ _____ V

$26 \div 2 =$ _____ C

$40 \div 2 =$ _____ B

$48 \div 6 =$ _____ R

$52 \div 2 =$ _____ S

$18 \div 2 =$ _____ T

$100 \div 10 =$ _____ H

$30 \div 2 =$ _____ A

$56 \div 8 =$ _____ N

___ ___ ___ ___ ___ ___ ___ ___ ___ ___ ___ ___ ___
 5   2   3   4   10   9   20   2   15   8   3   7   4

___ ___ ___ ___ ___ ___ ___ ___ ___ ___
15   13   9   3   14   3   9   3   2   26

From *Building Strong Bones & Muscles,* Graham Fishburne, Heather McKay, and Stephen Berg (2005). Champaign, IL: Human Kinetics.

ASSESSMENT TOOLS

As we mentioned in the beginning of this book, many of the weight-bearing exercises included in the circuits, games, dances, and gymnastics activities in this resource have been shown through research studies to produce significant positive changes in bones and muscles. Although the games and activities in this book have been designed to help develop strong bones and muscles, accurate assessment of bone and muscle development is not easy. Trained professionals are required to perform the intricate testing required to accurately determine the strength of bones and the growth and development of muscles. Such testing and measuring are beyond the scope of this book and the expectancy of instructors.

Physical Fitness Tests

One method of assessment that can be used to provide an indirect indication of bone strength and muscle strength is the standardized physical fitness tests for young children. Fitness tests can also provide indications of muscular endurance, cardiorespiratory efficiency, flexibility, agility, balance, and many other important areas associated with a child's growth and development. Professional associations such as AAHPERD (American Alliance for Health, Physical Education, Recreation and Dance) and CAHPERD (Canadian Association for Health, Physical Education, Recreation and Dance) provide guidance and recommendations on developmentally appropriate physical fitness tests for young children.

Other Learning Outcomes

In addition to bone and muscle development, as well as improvement in many areas of physical fitness, the activities in this resource promote many other desirable learning outcomes. The following checklists, tests, and quizzes provide ideas for ways to assess some of the learning outcomes associated with participation in the games and activities included in this book.

Assessment Checklists

The following checklists can serve as assessment guides for teachers and also be used as diagnostic teaching tools because they break down basic motor skills into component parts.

Observation Checklist for Fundamental Motor Skills

Name_____ Date_____

Place a check (√) in the box if a skill was observed and an X if a skill was not observed.

Forward Jumping—areas to observe	Jump 1	Jump 2	Jump 3
Arms are high and behind the body before the jump.			
Arms swing forward when jumping.			
Emphasis is placed on distance.			
Weight of the body is forward at landing.			

Leaping—areas to observe	Leap 1	Leap 2	Leap 3
Flow is relaxed and smooth.			
Takeoff leg is forceful.			
Legs are fully extended when off the ground.			

Hopping—areas to observe	Hop 1	Hop 2	Hop 3
Arms are used for force and not balance.			
Arms move together.			
There is a greater forward lean.			
The nonsupporting leg moves in time with other leg.			

Skipping—areas to observe	Skip 1	Skip 2	Skip 3
The whole body moves in a smooth, flowing action.			
There is little height on the hop.			
Landings are on the toes.			

Galloping—areas to observe	Gallop 1	Gallop 2	Gallop 3
The body moves in a smooth action.			
The trailing leg lands next to or behind the lead leg.			
The body is low to the ground when in the air.			

From *Building Strong Bones & Muscles,* Graham Fishburne, Heather McKay, and Stephen Berg (2005). Champaign, IL: Human Kinetics.

Movement Skills Checklist

1st Check _____(date)

2nd Check _____(date)

3rd Check _____(date)

Correct form (C) Incorrect form (I)

Student name	Jump			Leap			Hop			Skip			Gallop		
	1st check	2nd check	3rd check	1st check	2nd check	3rd check	1st check	2nd check	3rd check	1st check	2nd check	3rd check	1st check	2nd check	3rd check

From *Building Strong Bones & Muscles,* Graham Fishburne, Heather McKay, and Stephen Berg (2005). Champaign, IL: Human Kinetics.

Assessment of Stages of Motor Skill Development

Assessing children's fundamental motor skills is an important component of the elementary school physical education program. Fundamental motor skills can be broken down into three developmental phases: initial, elementary, and mature patterns of movement. Ideally, by the end of adolescence, all children under typical circumstances should be performing fundamental motor skills at a mature pattern of movement. The following provides an easy-to-use developmental assessment checklist of the locomotion skills that help produce muscle and bone development in children.

	Initial Stage	Elementary Stage	Mature Stage
Hopping	☐ Very little balance. ☐ May only do one or two hops. ☐ Little height or distance. ☐ Body appears rigid.	☐ Balance is better but is still not under control. ☐ May only do a few hops. ☐ Arms move bilaterally and very quickly. ☐ There is a slight forward lean.	☐ Arms are used for force and not balance. ☐ Arms move together. ☐ Greater forward lean. ☐ The nonsupporting leg moves in time with other leg.
Jumping	☐ Arms do not start the jumping action. ☐ Little emphasis placed on the length of the jump. ☐ Both feet may not be used at the same time for takeoff or landing. ☐ Body may fall backward at landing.	☐ Arms begin jumping action. ☐ Arms are at the front of the body before jump. ☐ Arms are used for balance in the air. ☐ There is a bigger crouch prior to the jump.	☐ Arms are high and behind the body before the jump. ☐ Arms swing forward when jumping. ☐ More emphasis placed on distance. ☐ Weight of the body is forward at landing.
Leaping	☐ Gains very little height and distance. ☐ Arms are not used very much. ☐ The takeoff leg is inconsistently used.	☐ Arms are mainly used for balance. ☐ Little height off of the ground. ☐ Legs are still quite bent when off the ground.	☐ Relaxed, smooth flow. ☐ Takeoff leg is forceful. ☐ Legs are fully extended when off the ground.
Skipping	☐ Arms are used very little. ☐ Skips on one foot. ☐ Stepping action instead of skip.	☐ Landing appears to be heavy or flat footed. ☐ Arms are better used to aid in skip. ☐ Step and hop are coordinated.	☐ Whole body moves in a smooth flowing action. ☐ Little height on the hop. ☐ Landings are on the toes.

From *Building Strong Bones & Muscles,* Graham Fishburne, Heather McKay, and Stephen Berg (2005). Champaign, IL: Human Kinetics.

Rubric for Assessing in the Area of Dance

Criteria	4 Excellent	3 Proficient	2 Adequate	1 Limited
Movement	Consistently performs sequence accurately and in rhythm	Usually performs accurately and in rhythm	Occasionally performs accurately and in rhythm	Rarely performs accurately and in rhythm
Dance formation	Consistently stays in formation for the entire dance	Frequently stays in formation for the entire dance	Occasionally stays in formation for the entire dance	Rarely stays in formation for the entire dance
Group coordination	Consistently coordinates moves with others	Frequently coordinates moves with others	Occasionally coordinates moves with others	Rarely coordinates moves with others

From *Building Strong Bones & Muscles*, Graham Fishburne, Heather McKay, and Stephen Berg (2005). Champaign, IL: Human Kinetics.

Knowledge and Attitude Assessment

Name_____ Date_____

Bone and Muscle Quiz

1. Name three foods that are high in calcium:

    1. _____

    2. _____

    3. _____

2. Name a type of exercise that strengthens your arm muscles:

    _____

3. What is the name of the disease that people have when their bones are weak and brittle?

    _____

4. Running, jumping, and hopping are what types of activities?

    _____

5. Is sitting in front of a television good or bad for making strong bones and muscles? Explain.

    _____

    _____

6. If you wanted to go swimming all the time to develop strong bones, would this be a good type of activity? Why or why not?

    _____

    _____

7. If you wanted to go swimming all the time to develop strong muscles, would this be a good activity? Why or why not?

    _____

    _____

From *Building Strong Bones & Muscles*, Graham Fishburne, Heather McKay, and Stephen Berg (2005). Champaign, IL: Human Kinetics.

Multiple Choice Questions

Circle the best response to the questions below. There is only one correct answer to each question.

1. What is osteoporosis?

   a. a bone injury
   b. a bone disease
   c. a bone infection
   d. a bone fracture

2. Which one of these activities is most effective for improving bone development?

   a. lifting weights
   b. swimming
   c. watching television
   d. playing cards

3. Which one of these activities provides strong muscles in your arms?

   a. push-ups
   b. sit-ups
   c. lunges
   d. running

4. Which one of the following beverages is a good source of calcium?

   a. coffee
   b. soda
   c. sport drinks
   d. milk

5. Which one of the following is a good weight-bearing activity?

   a. lying on the floor
   b. scuba diving
   c. swimming
   d. climbing a rope

6. What combination provides the best way to build strong bones and muscles?

   a. eating chips and playing computer games
   b. drinking milk and doing weight-bearing activity
   c. drinking sports drinks and watching sports
   d. eating chocolate bars and rollerblading

From *Building Strong Bones & Muscles*, Graham Fishburne, Heather McKay, and Stephen Berg (2005). Champaign, IL: Human Kinetics.

7. What food provides the best source of calcium?

    a. yogurt

    b. popcorn

    c. ham

    d. pretzels

8. Doing jumping jacks strengthens what area of the body?

    a. arms

    b. stomach

    c. head

    d. legs

9. If you do no activity, what will happen to your muscles?

    a. They will get bigger.

    b. They will get smaller.

    c. They will stay the same.

10. The best way to build strong bones and muscles is to

    a. do weight-bearing activities

    b. eat calcium-rich foods

    c. do nothing at all

    d. a and b

From *Building Strong Bones & Muscles,* Graham Fishburne, Heather McKay, and Stephen Berg (2005). Champaign, IL: Human Kinetics.

Knowledge and Attitude Assessment

1. Name three foods that are high in calcium.

   Milk

   Yogurt

   Cheese

2. Name a type of exercise that strengthens your arm muscles.

   Push-ups, chin-ups, swimming, gymnastics activities

3. What is the name of the disease that people have when their bones are weak and brittle?

   Osteoporosis

4. Running, jumping, and hopping are what types of activities?

   Weight-bearing

5. Is sitting in front of a television good or bad for making strong bones and muscles? Explain.

   Bad, because your body is at rest and your bones and muscles are inactive.

6. If you wanted to go swimming all the time to develop strong bones, would this be a good type of activity? Why or why not?

   No, because swimming is not a weight-bearing activity.

7. If you wanted to go swimming all the time to develop strong muscles, would this be a good activity? Why or why not?

   Yes, because the resistance from the water helps strengthen shoulders, arms, legs, and back muscles.

Multiple Choice Knowledge Questions

1-B; 2-A; 3-A; 4-D; 5-D; 6-B; 7-A; 8-D; 9-B; 10-D

From *Building Strong Bones & Muscles*, Graham Fishburne, Heather McKay, and Stephen Berg (2005). Champaign, IL: Human Kinetics.

Journal Entry

Journals can be used in several ways. For one thing, they can record thoughts and feelings about the experiences of a child. Journals can also be used for personal goal setting and to capture thoughts and reflections. The following is an example of an assignment for a journal entry.

In your journal, please respond to the following letter. You may use printed letters or handwriting; use correct spelling.

Dear Thomas,

You have been working really hard in our physical education classes on strengthening your muscles and bones. I hope that you have enjoyed the activities that we have been doing and that you have learned more about what it takes to have strong and healthy bones and muscles. I would like you to write in your journal a letter to your parents or guardians to share with them what you know about healthy bones and muscles and what you have been doing to make your bones and muscles strong. Tell them what your favorite activity was and what activities you do outside of the physical education class to help your bones and muscles grow strong. At the bottom of the page, draw a picture of an activity that makes your bones and muscles strong. Remember that you are writing a letter, so write in your natural voice.

Sincerely,
(teacher)

Scoring Rubric

1. Poor—journal is incomplete. Most questions are not answered; there are frequent spelling errors and poor writing. There is no drawing included or the drawing has little to do with strong bone or muscle development.

2. Marginal—journal is partially completed with very short answers. Writing is poor with some spelling errors. There is no drawing included or the drawing has little to do with strong bone or muscle development. The drawing lacks color or neatness.

3. Good—journal is completed with most questions answered in a narrative format. Writing is clear with very few spelling mistakes. The drawing provides a good example of an activity that develops strong bones and muscles. The drawing is colorful and neat.

4. Excellent—journal is completed with all questions answered in a narrative format. Writing is very clear, with no spelling mistakes. The drawing provides a very good example of an activity that develops strong bones and muscles. The drawing is colorful and neat.

From *Building Strong Bones & Muscles*, Graham Fishburne, Heather McKay, and Stephen Berg (2005). Champaign, IL: Human Kinetics.

ACHIEVEMENT RECOGNITION AND MOTIVATION

The games and activities in this resource have been designed to help children develop strong bones and muscles. However, to maintain strong bones and muscles, regular participation in the activities is necessary. Instructors should take it on themselves to help motivate children to develop active, healthy lifestyles. Children need to be motivated to participate in high-impact weight-bearing activities outside of school time. To sustain motivation, they also need to be recognized for their efforts. What follows are some ideas to help children develop activities beyond the school environment and to recognize them for their efforts. The first item, the Bone and Muscle Calendar, is an activity children can do at home to help build strong bones and muscles. In the remaining materials in this appendix you will find recognition certificates to help reward and motivate children throughout the year.

Dear parent(s),

The physical education classes that your child has been taking recently have been focusing on making bones and muscles stronger through a variety of activities both in and out of the gym. Research has shown that children who do weight-bearing activities such as jumping and skipping increase their bone density, which helps prevent bone loss later in their life. Although we have been working on this in our physical education classes, we need your help!

Having your child perform some weight-bearing activities at home will really help him or her build strong bones and muscles. The calendar provided indicates a weight-bearing activity for every day of the month. Ask your child to demonstrate some of the activities we have been doing. Better yet, be a role model and participate along with your child. You might see the benefits as well! I hope that these activities will help your child develop positive learning habits to stay active and healthy.

Sincerely,
(teacher)

From *Building Strong Bones & Muscles,* Graham Fishburne, Heather McKay, and Stephen Berg (2005). Champaign, IL: Human Kinetics.

Bone and Muscle Calendar

Although the calendar activities take very little time to do, the benefits you will see at the end of the month will be significant. Try to perform at least 20 of these activities. Have one of your parents initial the calendar each day you have performed an activity. Better yet, ask your parents to do the activities with you! At the end of the month, bring your calendar to class. Remember—build your bones and strengthen those muscles!

Sunday	Monday	Tuesday	Wednesday	Thursday	Friday	Saturday
Do 1 minute of Leaping Lizards	25 Jumping jacks	10 Push-ups	Gallop around the yard	Seal Crawl around the kitchen floor	Do 10 one-foot jumps on each leg	10 Sit-ups
Coffee Grinder both ways	Crab Walk around the living room	Jog on the spot for 1 minute	Wall sit for 30 seconds	Jump rope for 2 minutes	10 Frog Jumps in the yard	10 Push-ups
Play a game of hopscotch	Lame Puppy Walk around the house	10 Tuck Jumps	10 Sit-ups	Do 1 minute of Leaping Lizards	Bear Walk around the yard	Do 10 one-foot jumps on each leg
25 Jumping jacks	Inchworm the length of your bedroom	Crab Walk around the living room	Jump rope for 2 minutes	10 Push-ups	Seal Crawl around the kitchen floor	10 Tuck Jumps
10 Frog Jumps in the yard	Jog on the spot for 1 minute	10 Two-foot vertical jumps	Slither like a snake around your bedroom	Do 10 jumps as high as you can in your yard	Hop on each leg for 20 seconds; rest and do it again	**WAY TO GO!**

From *Building Strong Bones & Muscles,* Graham Fishburne, Heather McKay, and Stephen Berg (2005). Champaign, IL: Human Kinetics.

Certificate of Recognition

This is to recognize that

_____

has done an outstanding job in performing weight-bearing activities that contribute to healthy bones and muscles.

Great Job!

From *Building Strong Bones & Muscles*, Graham Fishburne, Heather McKay, and Stephen Berg (2005). Champaign, IL: Human Kinetics.

Make No Bones About It

This is to certify that

_____

has helped develop strong bones and muscles by performing weight-bearing activities and eating healthy foods.

Great Job!

From *Building Strong Bones & Muscles*, Graham Fishburne, Heather McKay, and Stephen Berg (2005). Champaign, IL: Human Kinetics.

Student of the Month

This is to certify that

_____

understands and demonstrates the importance of exercising and eating healthy foods that will help develop strong bones and muscles.

Great Job!

From *Building Strong Bones & Muscles*, Graham Fishburne, Heather McKay, and Stephen Berg (2005). Champaign, IL: Human Kinetics.

REFERENCES AND RESOURCES

Allen, L. (1997). *Physical activity ideas for action: Elementary level.* Champaign, IL: Human Kinetics.

Bailey, D.A., Faulkner, R.A., & McKay, H.A. (1996). Growth, physical activity, and bone mineral acquisition. *Exercise Sport Science Review,* 24, 233-266.

Burk, M.C. (2002). *Station games: Fun and imaginative PE lessons.* Champaign, IL: Human Kinetics.

Faigenbaum, A., & Westcott, W. (2000). *Strength and power training for young athletes.* Champaign, IL: Human Kinetics.

Fishburne, G.J. (2005). *Developmentally appropriate physical education for children and youth.* Edmonton, Alberta: Ripon Publishing.

Grineski, S. (1996). *Cooperative learning in physical education.* Champaign, IL: Human Kinetics.

Hacker, P., Malmberg, E., & Nance, J. (1996). *Gymnastics fun and games: 51 activities for children.* Champaign, IL: Human Kinetics.

Hanrahan, S.J., & Carlson, T.B. (2000). *Game skills: A fun approach to learning sport skills.* Champaign, IL: Human Kinetics.

Khan, K., McKay, H., Kannus, P., Bailey, D., Wark, J., & Bennell, K. (2001). *Physical activity and bone health.* Champaign, IL: Human Kinetics.

Kirchner, G., & Fishburne, G.J. (1998). *Physical education for elementary school children* (10th ed.). New York: McGraw-Hill.

MacKelvie, K., McKay, H., Petit, M., Moran, O., & Khan, K. (2002). Bone mineral response to a 7-month randomized controlled, school-based jumping intervention in 121 prepubertal boys: Associations with ethnicity and body mass index. *Journal of Bone Mineral Research,* 17, 834-844.

McKay, H., Tsang, G., Heinonen, A., MacKelvie, K., Sanderson, D., & Khan, K. (2005). Ground reaction forces associated with an effective elementary school based jumping intervention. *British Journal of Sports Medicine,* 39, 10-14.

McKay, H.A., & Khan, K.M. (2000). Bone mineral acquisition during childhood and adolescence: Physical exercise as a preventative measure. In Henderson, J.E., & Goltzman, D. (Eds.), *The osteoporosis primer.* Cambridge University Press, Cambridge, U.K., 179-185.

McKay, H.A., Petit, M.A., Schutz, R.W., Prior, J.C., Barr, S.I., & Khan, K.M. (2000). Augmented trochanteric bone mineral density after modified physical education classes: A randomized school-based exercise intervention study in prepubescent and early pubescent children. *Journal of Pediatrics,* 136(2), 156-162.

Osteoporosis Society of Canada (2004). *About osteoporosis: What is osteoporosis?* (http://www.osteoporosis.ca)

U.S. Surgeon General's Report (2004). *Bone health and osteoporosis: A report of the Surgeon General,* October 14, 2004. U.S. Department of Health and Human Services. (http://www.surgeongeneral.gov/library/bonehealth/factsheet1.html)

ABOUT THE AUTHORS

Graham Fishburne, PhD, is a professor of education at the University of Alberta. He is recognized as an international leader in the world's "Who's Who in Sport Pedagogy Theory and Research" and has received numerous research and teaching awards, including the Canadian National Teaching Award as one of Canada's top teachers. His major areas of expertise are in children's motor development and effective teaching. Professor Fishburne has authored many books and articles on elementary school physical education and has 30 years of teaching experience at all levels of school and university education. He is an internationally recognized educator, and is regularly consulted by government agencies to offer advice and leadership on developmentally appropriate physical education programs for children and youth, and to offer guidance on the most effective programs for teacher training and professional development.

Heather McKay, PhD, is a professor in the departments of orthopaedics and family practice at the University of British Columbia. A Michael Smith Foundation for Health Research senior scholar, Dr. McKay is internationally recognized for her research related to physical activity and children's health and their applications in community and school settings. Dr. McKay cofounded ActionSchools BC! (www.actionschoolsbc.ca) in partnership with numerous community and government stakeholders.

Stephen Berg, MEd, is a graduate student in the department of elementary education at the University of Alberta and a member of the Canadian Association of Health, Physical Education, Recreation and Dance. He has received two university teaching awards for excellence in undergraduate teaching and has taught K-12 physical education. He currently teaches undergraduate courses in elementary school physical education curriculum and instruction. He is doing his PhD work on effective delivery of a healthy bone program in elementary schools.

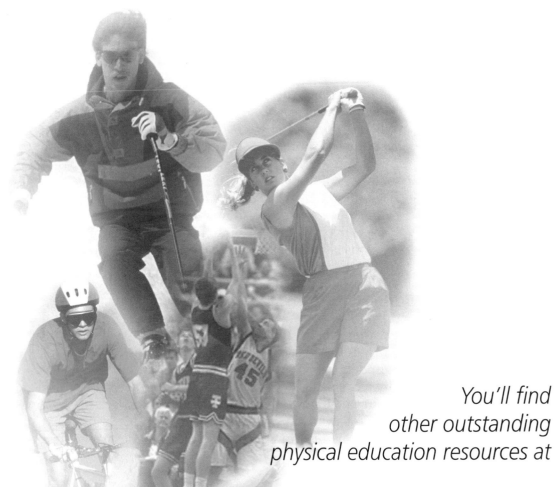